Understanding What Just Happened to You

UNDERSTANDING WHAT JUST HAPPENED TO YOU!

THE ULTIMATE GUIDE

TO UNDERSTANDING SALVATION

AFC, DR. PAUL VICKERS

Understanding What Just Happened To You!

THE ULTIMATE GUIDE TO UNDERSTANDING SALVATION

ISBN: **978-0-9600947-0-7**

ISBN: **978-0-9600947-0-7**

Library of congress Control Number: *Registration #: TXU-142-092*

Print information available from:

Published date: August 31st 2019

-Endorsement and my Respect-

There is nothing more confusing than religion. It is at the foundation of most of our global conflicts today and continues to be a challenge to the brightest of minds. History is filled with records of the tremendous impact religion has had on so many lives, cultures, nations and civilizations. Religion is the single most powerful influence on the development of humanity since the beginning.

Because of the vital roles religion plays in the life of the human journey, it is critical that we understand what we believe and how that belief impacts on our perception of life for ourselves and others. There are many religions in the world, each one claiming to have the right answers to life both here and hereafter. However, the biblical concepts of the spiritual answers to the questions of the heart of mankind are the most reasonable, logical and complete.

In this work, ***Understanding What Just Happened to You,"*** Paul Vickers provides us with one of the most comprehensive discourse on the acceptance, reacceptance, appropriation and development of a walk of faith in Christ Jesus and the biblical redemption. His simple, yet profoundly sound approach to a very broad subject gives you a mountain top view of the many parts of the process that could be a maze of spiritual concepts. Covering such topics as what it means to Repent, Born Again, Saved and Converted and a multitude of other foundational principles of the kingdom life, makes this book an owner's manual for spiritual development and growth.

I highly recommend this work as a necessary tool for the counselor and the new converts. It provides the basics for living a successful kingdom citizen. Read on and enjoy the journey to the best in The Kingdom of God.

-Dr. Myles E Munroe, *Nassau Bahamas, April 1954 –Nov. 2014*

Introduction

Greetings in the wonderful name of Jesus the Christ who is God's one and only begotten son. "***Who being the brightness of his glory, and the express image of his person...***" Hebrews 1:3. The purpose for writing this book stems from my conversations with both Biblical leaders as well as non-religious people. There are vast differences each sector upholds, even of the same denomination; especially on the subject matters of salvation, God's Holy Spirit and even resurrection.

God's plan of salvation is to re-establish an intimate one-on-one relationship to the same degree He had with Adam in the Garden of Eden a little over 6,000 years ago. Therefore, God's desire is to rekindle a right relationship with all of His offspring. ***See Genesis 2:19-22***. However, this type of communion cannot be properly experienced today unless we believe and understand more about His precise plan surrounding salvation and our personal make-up. God's Word will meet anyone where they are presently and provide a clear path of understanding of the reason for their life and their purpose.

"***Just as He chose us in Him before the foundation of the world, that we should be holy and without blame before Him in love***. " Ephesians 1:4. We are never to become complacent where we are in the Lord because He has a never-ending flow of revelation for each of His offspring. Depending on age and level of maturity in God, each Scripture can take on a higher meaning not a different meaning. This is through revelation.

Revelation is not just the unveiling of something previously unknown. It is a higher exposure to God's Word we may have read, believed or employed. Then, it can take believers to an even higher plateau based on their close communion with His Holy Spirit. "***How that by revelation He made known to me the mystery (as I have briefly written already, by which, when you read, you may understand my knowledge in the mystery of Christ), which in other ages was not made known to the sons of men, as it has now been <u>revealed by the Spirit</u> to His holy apostles and prophets***." Ephesians 3:3-5. Therefore, the Word of God does not mean different things to different people as you may have heard/been taught. "***For God is not the author of***

confusion, but of peace, as in all churches of the saints." I Corinthians 14:33 God's Holy Spirit is called the Spirit of truth. "***However, when He, the Spirit of truth, has come, He will guide you into all truth…"*** John 16:13. The Word of God confirms that He is always accessible to guide anyone into reality and new heights of comprehension when they choose to acknowledge Him as the ultimate instructor. The most distinguishing section in the entire Word of God is detailed in **Matthew 17:1-9**.

These series of verses clearly identify that Jesus is above Moses who represented The Law and Elijah who represented all the prophets. God had to specify this particular occurrence in plain sight for us in order to demonstrate Jesus' superiority; it also reflected His status, excellence and the vast difference He makes because He was indeed God Himself expressed in the flesh. "***For in Him dwells all the fullness of the Godhead bodily***." Colossians 2:9. God desires us to know His **only** begotten Son/The Christ, *–who could not be or was ever Michael the archangel–* but The Savior who could die, raise Himself so that He could redeem man back to His Father and God. "***Therefore God, Your God, has anointed You with the oil of gladness more than Your companions***." Hebrews 1:9. Also, did you know Jesus said, "***all that ever came before me are thieves and robbers: but the sheep did not hear them***." John 10:8. What does this verses mean, indicate and convey? It is crystal clear that no one before Jesus got it right. Therefore, God had to come in the flesh *–Jesus–* to be the ultimate example –**The God/Man**– to show us what authority we have as spirit beings living in a physical body. Jesus is the **only** separator and the single distinguishing factor throughout the entire Word of Truth. Finally, He is really the Unprecedented One and extremely rare commodity throughout the entire Word of Truth.

The reason we are making these monumental statements and provide supporting Scriptural evidence is that there is no other way to God. Jesus said, "***I am the way, the truth, and the life. No one comes to the Father except through Me***." John 14:6. There is no equal nor ever will be! In other words, if Jesus made a statement and someone else whether prior to or after said something contrary, we are to ONLY vie for Him. This means we adhere to and believe what Jesus said as accurate, true and concrete compared to absolutely everyone else!

Information→ The Word of Truth ←Warning

Beloved, there is a very subtle and seamlessly harmless word we use rampantly today to describe events written in God's eternal Word. This watered-down term is ~~'story'~~ which should **NEVER** be used when ministering or teaching others about the encounters in God's Word. '**Story**' is defined as a real or imaginary account told for entertainment. As believers, we know there is NOTHING written in God's Word for entertainment. Did you know the word 'story' refers to a fairy-tale? **God's entire Library** of sixty-six (**66**) books is about The King, His vast kingdom and His children; it refers to itself as:

1-- **Covenant**
2-- **Law of God**
3-- **Gospel of God**
4-- **The Good News**
5-- **The Word of God**
6-- **Treaty /Testament**
7-- **The Word of Truth**
8-- **Sword of The Spirit**
9-- **Doctrine of The Lord**
10--**The Will of The Lord**
11- **The Word of The Gospel**
12--**The Everlasting Covenant**
13--**The Words of Eternal Life**
14--**The Doctrine of God our Savior**

Also, God provides us with four replacement words which we use to create a great acronym for easy memorization. The acronym spells the word **T.E.A.M** which opposes the word ~~story~~. TEAM unveils a:

T-eaching which is mentioned **25** times in Scripture
E-xample which is mentioned **8** times
A-ccount is mentioned **17** times and
M-essage is mentioned **7** times.

God's Word is **not** fiction but an 'instruction manual' about The **Godhead** mentioned only three (**3**) times. Finally, it details the origin of life on earth, who we are and the expectation of righteous living in anticipation of eternal life in the New Jerusalem.

TABLE OF CONTENT

Chapter 1----------→ *Repent*

Foundation Concepts 101

Let us embark and set sail on a brief but detailed journey towards a clearer understanding of God's plan of salvation. We would like you to picture yourself on an exploration vessel at the surface of the clear but deep waters of God's Word. You can begin to feel excited because you are about to begin your descent into a vast ocean of knowledge. Your tour guide *–who can always be relied upon–* is God's awesome Holy Spirit who is fully aware of all the things which you will see, marvel and desire to know more about. He is The Ultimate Teacher!

Whether you are a new, mature or a vacillating believer on this expedition, the Holy Spirit is available to equip and sustain you. This is so that you look forward to learning new principles from both the natural means and His spiritual unveiling. "***But the natural man does not receive the things of the Spirit of God, for they are foolishness to him; nor can he know them, because they are spiritually discerned.***" I Corinthians 2:14.

All who are identified with Christ by their confession of faith are being steered towards understanding their ambassador's assignment on earth. This is just one of many designations applied to believers throughout this exciting life's expedition in the salvation process.

On this outing, God provides those young in Him with the appropriate nourishment needed for steady growth. God's Word says, "***As <u>newborn</u> babes, desire the pure milk of the word that you may grow thereby***." I Peter 2:2. If we acknowledge the Holy Spirit in the things of God, He will move us from any murky **carnal mindset** to the **clear spiritual** outlook in the new direction we are heading. "***For to be carnally minded is death, but to be spiritually minded is life and peace.***" Romans 8:6. "***And I, brethren, could not speak to you as to spiritual people but as to carnal, as to babes in Christ***" I Corinthians 3:1. God desires us to grow from being babies in Christ to becoming mature stewards. "***Let a man so account of us, as of the ministers of***

Christ, and stewards of the mysteries of God"1 Corinthians 4:1. These are focused and dedicated believers who choose to become equipped so they can properly manage God's affairs as stewards on earth. This is the arena where they can begin dining on solid food. "***But solid food is for the mature, who because of practice have their senses trained to discern good and evil.***" Hebrews 5:14. Also, these are believers who are able to discern between doing good things and doing the right things which are acceptable by God's standard. Through a close communion with His Holy Spirit, anyone can become acute to distinguish between sin and iniquity, partially devoted or fully **committed** believer. By the way to **commit** means to:

C-hange
O-ld
M-ind-set &
M-ove
I-nto
T-riumph

As we grow and increase in knowledge, some will realize there were constant prayers made by a concerned friend, loving family member or an insightful colleague that were answered just so your seat of the salvation journey could be reserved. Others will recognize God did make their reservation for this new expedition before the foundations of the world.

"***According as he hath chosen us in him before the foundation of the world, that we should be holy and without blame before him in love: having predestinated us unto the adoption of children by Jesus Christ to himself, according to the good pleasure of his will.***" Ephesians 1:4-5.

Again, this vessel some chose to board is designed to take them towards a clearer comprehension of salvation so they can easily convey to others their unique salvation experience. There is no greater miracle than salvation when someone chooses to come to God through Christ. The Word confirms, "…***of which salvation the prophets have enquired and searched diligently, who prophesied of the grace that should come unto you.***" 1 Peter 1:10.

Even the angels of God desire to look into salvation as well. "*...**they were ministering the things which now have been reported to you through those who have preached the gospel to you by the Holy Spirit sent from heaven—things which angels desire to look into.***"1 Peter 1:12. As you grow deeper in knowledge *–which is information–* you will begin to realize the key people God placed in our lives years ago, just so you could be guided and have now arrived where God knew you would be today.

One of God's ultimate goal for all of us is, "*...**till we all come to the unity of the faith and of the knowledge of the Son of God, to a perfect man, to the measure of the stature of the fullness of Christ."*** Ephesians 4:13. God's Word tell us, "***And be kind to one another, tenderhearted, forgiving one another, even as God in Christ forgave you***." Ephesians 4:32. However, in order for us to come into His light of revelation, the Scripture says there is something each of us are to do. "***And do not be conformed to this world, but be transformed by the renewing of your mind, that you may prove what is that good and acceptable and perfect will of God."*** Romans 12:2.

As a newborn, we are not to re-engage in the things of the world because we are born into a different family lineage. In essence, we may have to leave the port of conformity, some friends and those not heading in your direction of Christ's teachings to now fully commit to follow Christ. Please sit back and enjoy the ride into a plethora of understanding God's marvelous and intricate plan of salvation. You are now in first class seating which has been reserved exclusively for you.

Clearly Defining What It Means to Repent

The primary focus in this section specifically outlines **repent**: The word repent is a very interesting word. It is used by God in His plan towards initiating a sequence of progressive changes. From a Scriptural standpoint, repent means to think differently and to reconsider. In other words, change your thinking; turn around your thoughts and focus them in God's direction.

Also, it involves a mental reconstruction which should result in a new change in attitude. There has to be evidence of growth in your new life because God now lives in you. And, He does expect measurable progress within a reasonable amount of time. We are to change our psychology or state of mind. This is why repent is an all-encompassing word directed to our mindset. Repent means to:

R-eturn *to*
E-lohim *who*
P-rovides
E-ternal-*life*
N-ewness &
T-ransformation

Even though He provides newness and transformation, we are the ones who choose to open the door and let Him in. Let us bring things closer to home by providing other familiar terms surrounding repent. In our English language, repent is a word which is made up of a prefix ***RE*** and a word ***PENT***. *RE* means again; *PENT* means a high place. Together, '*RE*' and '*PENT*' denote a restoration to a previous place, position or status.

For example, let us use a very familiar word to clearly convey what repent means; it is the word '**re**-turn.' We know it means to go back to an earlier place. We cannot return to a place we've never been. Relatively, repent signifies we are entitled to occupy an original high place which was God's original plan for His creation. Beloved, did you know God created humans to live forever?

Let us disclose an even greater understanding of '**pent**' using a relevant compound word, 'pent-house'. A penthouse is a house at the top or roof of a building. The combination of the modern definition 'repent' and the spiritual description amplifies the true significance and the weight God really intended repent to convey.

God's plan of salvation is to restore the original status to the same prominence He had with Adam and Eve before they fell away spiritually. Did you know repent is relevant in our everyday lives today? For example, we encounter terms or systems which constantly reminds us to; **'re-pent'** or change our direction. For example, in our armed forces or U.S Military they use the term, "**about face**" to their Privates –PVT– which are new recruits. Then, at our local DMV or Department of Motor Vehicle, before we are given a license to operate a vehicle, an instructor requires us to make a proper **"U-Turn"** on your road test. Also, the way we define when someone has made a significant change in their personal life, we say they did a "**one hundred eighty-degree turn.**"

All three changes are designed to alter our direction so that we experience new scenery. This way, we can obey commands, drive safer, and make stops without having accidents wherever we turn. However, these simple compilations mean that we have to **deny** ourselves of our own direction and choose to go/do something new or different. When we deny ourselves, it means to:

D-eprive
E-go &
N-eglect
Y-ourself

You cannot serve God and yourself equally. The Scripture confirms; "***No man can serve two masters: for either he will hate the one, and love the other***..." Matthew 6:24. In the New Treaty, when John the Baptist *-Jesus' forerunner-* cried out, 'repent for the kingdom of heaven arrived', he was alerting and awakening the people to something brand new. John's message was to redirect their thoughts from what was familiar. This message was directed to everyone including the religious Scribes, Pharisees, Herodian and Sadducees. By adhering to his message, it would prepare them for the arrival of Jesus' new administration. You see saint, God wanted to introduce a new and superior covenant which has better promises. **See Hebr. 8:6**.

The Association between Repenting and Believing

Even though there are four terms which describe what salvation entails, it is the hearing of God's Word and acting upon it which causes someone to repent. This is the natural order of progression towards obtaining eternal salvation. Fundamentally, repent hinges on believing. Just as a fire needs oxygen to prolong burning, repent also requires your belief in order to keep working. After someone believes and agrees Jesus is Lord, their spirit is rekindled, stamped with God's approval and identified with Christ. This means there is a mark placed on each believer's spirit by His Holy Spirit showing ownership. "***In Him you also trusted, after you heard the word of truth, the gospel of your salvation; in whom also, having believed, you were sealed with the Holy Spirit of promise.*"** Ephesians 1:13.

Also, in Mark's account of the Gospel, he mentioned when Jesus came into Galilee preaching the Good News of the kingdom of God what it would accomplish. "***Repent and believe the gospel***." Mark 1:15. Jesus' objective was to redirect their thought life away from what they were focused on; like traditions, rituals and ceremonies so they would return to God using the right track of salvation.

This new mindset would begin to bring them out of their own prior misconceptions about God *–whom they thought they knew–* to a new and more meaningful status. As far as Jesus was concerned, without repenting they were living, but not plugged into their Source who is their Father God. It is God's plan that we become alive again unto Him because all human beings *–no matter how proper they try to live apart from God–* are still separated from Him by Adam's original sin nature. The reason why God sent His Son was to redeem/buy back mankind to Him. God is letting us know we are not able to obtain salvation on our own works/merits.

If we could obtain it on our own, we would not need the Savior Jesus the Christ. Our adversary *–the devil–* began his series of actions against humans by first hindering and then darkening the awareness all humans are born with towards the reality of God's presence in their daily lives. This, in–part, was a choice everyone made to live a separated or a lukewarm lifestyle. Some of us are busy strolling through life in the middle of the road not realizing it is the most dangerous place to be. "***But if our gospel be hid, it is hid to them that are lost: In whom the god of this world hath blinded the minds of***

them which believe not, lest the light of the glorious gospel of Christ, who is the image of God should shine unto them. " 2 Cor. 4:3-4.

God has now made the light of the glorious gospel of His Son available to shine into man's alienated minds. Question! How can the adversary blind the minds of people towards God? Does he have the right? If so, who gave him that right? God surely didn't! Blindness, which is the absence of light; and darkness, which is the absence of knowledge, comes on the scene as a result of our own choice of unbelief. The light of the glorious gospel of Christ *–as previously mentioned–* shines into darkened minds so God's light can be evident.

You see saints, the enemy can blind the minds of those who choose **<u>not</u>** to believe God's Word about what they have heard. Unbelief stems from the decision people make to hold on to the old rituals and traditions. Hence the reason why it is so critical for people when they hear the New Treaty's arrangement, they are to take action. This is so that the process of repenting can be set in motion right away.

We are about to unveil another premiere spiritual truth. In order for the enemy to dim our paths or darken our minds, a spiritual law is usually violated. This is the time when the enemy's actual rights begin. **<u>If</u>** it was left entirely up to the devil, everyone would be walking in darkness or dead which is obviously not the case. As we are all aware, there are consequences for violating our earthly laws. By the same token, if we do <u>not</u> choose to believe God's written spiritual laws when we are aware of it, we will violate God's spiritual decree. Since God's Word is spirit ***–John 6:63–*** it must carry spiritual effects whether good or bad. This seems so simple and plain.

In fact, when anyone chooses to act positively, we allow God's light to open our understanding. The immediate effect is that we begin to think differently about His Word. However, if we constantly revisit sin, hold on to unforgiveness or embrace various lust, it will allow the enemy the right to deflect the light of understanding which God is shining towards us. Again, there is always a consequence for violating laws just as there is inner peace when we adhere to God's Truth. We are never to allow any particular denomination, affiliation or religious sects to limit our pursuit of God. We are to be like the Bereans of old who "…***searched the Scriptures daily to see if those things are so.***"

Acts 17:10-11. Ultimate truth can only be revealed and confirmed by God's Holy Spirit, not man's teaching. "***But the anointing which you have received from Him abides in you, and you do not need that anyone teach you; but as the same anointing teaches you concerning all things, and is true, and is not a lie, and just as it has taught you, you will abide in Him.***"1 John 2:27.

The Association Between Repent and Baptism

"In those days John the Baptist came preaching in the wilderness of Judea, and saying, "Repent, for the kingdom of heaven is at hand." Matthew 3:1-2. In order to gain a proper understanding of this verse, let us examine it from both Jesus' perspective and from John the Baptist's position. John said, ***I indeed baptize you with water unto repentance, but He who is coming after me is mightier than I, whose sandals I am not worthy to carry. He will baptize you with the Holy Spirit and fire.*** Matthew 3:11.

Please note, there are two available types of baptisms. However, we will only be addressing the first one which engulfs water as it supports only the salvation experience. We want to point out that water baptism is not mandatory in order to obtain salvation but recommended. Water baptism is a natural requirement which fulfills a spiritual purpose. Also, it should result in having a clear conscience towards God. ***Corresponding to that, baptism now saves you— not the removal of dirt from the flesh, but an appeal to God for a good conscience— through the resurrection of Jesus Christ.*** I Peter 3:21.

Water baptism is necessary in order to equip new believers with a right conscience towards God; whereas, the other baptism is about obtaining more spiritual authority, an in-filling and a new but unfamiliar prayer dialect. Romans 8:26-27. To take water baptism a step further, the Scripture said, "***Then Jesus came from Galilee to John at the Jordan to be baptized by him. And John tried to prevent Him, saying, "I need to be baptized by You, and are You coming to***

me?" Matthew 3:13. While Jesus was here physically for thirty-three and a half years, *–who was God in the flesh–* He did not object to this seemingly natural, earthly undertaking; He humbled Himself to fulfill a deed of righteousness and to be our example. Beloved, to be water baptized does not mean to sprinkle, dip or hose-down, but to immerse and cover. This is why when John was providing this Godly recommendation for the people he did so where there was a lot of water. ***And John also was baptizing in Aenon near to Salim, because there was much water there: and they came, and were baptized.*** John 3:23.

Without complicating what water baptism is all about, it is simply dying to our old self and us rising in Christ to a new and more meaningful outlook towards God. ***Therefore, we were buried with Him through baptism into death, that just as Christ was raised from the dead by the glory of the Father, even so we also should walk in newness of life.*** Romans 6:4. It is important that water baptism follows a new believer's commitment on the day or soon after they confess Jesus as Lord to assist in their identification with Him.

Please remember to write-down the date as a point of reference for your own recollection when ministering to others. It is good to note after we have been baptized we may not feel, look or be different outwardly. What is important is that we are being obedient to God's directive which, by the way, is the only evidence that shows we love Him. For additional information about baptism, you can study the encounter between Phillip and the Ethiopian Eunuch. ***See Acts 8:26-40.*** You will notice the Eunuch requested baptism even before Phillip mentioned it. Also ***Acts 19:1-8***.

What Is Repentance?

As strange as the following statement may be to some, it is *not* intended to be a play on words. Neither is it meant to tamper with the English language. However, there are times in Scripture when REPENT and REPENTANCE take on two different applications. Our intent is only to help broaden the overall understanding of just how far God has gone to open the portal of returning to Him. There are several times when repent is used, as *–what we know today is–* a noun. Repentance takes on an entirely different direction in relationship to salvation. "***For it is impossible for those who were once enlightened, and have tasted the heavenly gift, and have become partakers of the Holy Spirit, and have tasted the good word of God and the powers of the age to come,*** [6] ***if they fall away, to renew them again to repentance, since they crucify again for themselves the Son of God, and put Him to an open shame***." Hebrews 6:4-6. According to this Scripture, repentance pertains to mature children of God who were once on track but have derailed themselves despite knowing better. The more familiar parallel used today is "**back-slid**." This is when a believer **re**visits and basks in the pleasures of this world they once enjoyed.

The underlined word above 'again' is key. There is a three-fold idea behind repentance which involves the touching of the intellect, the returning to their Source and the determination to walk in right standings before God and people. Did you know that God our Father even went the extra mile to provide His children with a way back to Him? Even though they were led back by their own "***the lust of the flesh, lust of the eyes and the pride of life***"– 1 John 2:16. The Scripture tells us how this privilege and opportunity was made available. It is by God's agape love *–without reason–* for His children. "***Not knowing that the goodness of God leads you to repentance?***" Romans 2:4. Then, it states what has to take place in order for repentance to work. "…***For godly sorrow produces repentance leading to salvation, not to be regretted***." II Corinthians 7:10.

Please be aware, no one can have godly sorrow unless they had previous ties and a close relationship. Most of us today can easily relate to 'close ties' if we think about all the great things our parents or guardians have done for us. The verse *–mentioned above–* is not directed to the world, but to backsliders and those who chose to go back–and–forth or dabble. The detour some will make is a deliberate and conscious act to revisit the pleasures of sin which will bring an open shame to Christ. Also, those associated with the ones who fall can be faced with mockery and even ridicule by the authorities or critics of our faith. You see saint, after someone has been introduced to God's Word and incorporated His principles as the standard to their interactions in life, if or when they do fall back into the debaucheries of this world's appeals, at some point they will realize they really do not belong there. The prodigal son, for example, is probably the best case and detailed account we can reference. It is stated in Luke chapter fifteen. Those who fall back will remember some major occurrence in their life when they knew they were better-off with God. And, others will recall how they were miraculously delivered from danger, arrest or even death.

This awareness can bring about Godly sorrow which is needed in order to transport them back on the right track or once familiar road. The realization is the things about God they believed, acted upon and experienced were all true. And, when they revisited the state of sinful pleasures, they knew they needed a one hundred and eighty-degree turn to the Father and His Son Jesus. Rest assured, if they continued on that free-way of deception and ignored God's provision of reconciliation *–His goodness–* they would suffer the consequence for their neglect. ***See Matthew 7:13-29.***

Since God's provision is in place, they can act upon His outstretched arms *–provisions–* as Peter and the prodigal son came to find out. If either one would have remained off course, it could have eventually resulted in an eternal separation from Him. The Scriptures alert us today of God's extended love. It says He is, "…***not willing that any should perish but that all should come unto repentance***." II Peter 3:9. God does not want any of His blood-bought children to revisit sin, especially after coming into the proper light and new knowledge of the truth; He simply wants His children to be aware of the additional cost for reconciliation.

This is like the price parents pay to get their child(ren) out of jail, trouble and arrest. God's concern for His offspring reaches both the lost and the mature to let them comprehend the vastness of His love which goes far above and beyond all human comprehension. "***For God so loved the world that he gave his only begotten Son, that whosoever believeth in him should not perish, but have everlasting life***." John 3:16. Whether someone has confessed Jesus as Lord for the first time or has strayed off course, provisions are still available. As we mentioned, there will be an additional expense. Therefore, as similar as repent is to repentance may seem to be, repentance seems to be at another plateau …" ***If they shall fall away, to renew them again unto repentance; seeing they crucify to themselves the Son of God afresh, and put him to an open shame.*** " Hebrews 6:6.

A Godly Parallel about September 11th, 2001

We were all shocked, devastated and angry at the tragedies of September 11th, 2001. And, most of us who lived through it either verbally or unconsciously asked, why? Why did these tragedies occur? We then reasoned within ourselves and questioned why didn't God prevent it? Hundreds of families, relatives, friends, loved ones, innocent lives and businesses suffered devastating losses of epic proportions and jobs were lost or shut down as a result.

We are also to begin incorporating God more in all our endeavors realizing life is not only short but also unpredictable. There is a relevant example in Scripture when lives were lost because an unforeseen disaster occurred killing numerous religious priests who were worshipping God at the time. This devastation took place when the **tower** *–a building in Jerusalem–* collapsed killing all those within. It was interesting that when Jesus mentioned this account, He did not attempt to provide an answer as to why this calamity occurred, but more-so, he placed a very high emphasis only on man's need to **repent**.

Jesus' response alerted everyone's conscience, preconceptions and religious beliefs to the present disaster. He went on to say, "***do you think they were worse sinners than all other men who dwell in Jerusalem, I tell you no, but unless you <u>repent</u> you will all likewise perish."*** Luke 13:4-5. There are two primary commandments we have towards God and man. "***Jesus said to him, you shall love the LORD your God with all your <u>heart</u>, with all your <u>soul</u>, and with all your <u>mind</u>. This is the first and great commandment. And the second is like it: You shall love your neighbor as yourself.*** " Matthew 22:37-39.

In other words, we all need a heart transplant. As ambassadors for Christ, we have to wake up to the reality that tragedies can occur anywhere, anytime and to anyone. However, God does not ordain them; neither is He responsible for innocent lives that are lost as a result of occurrences. God simply knows all things that are going to happen which makes Him God! This should be a good reason why we are to stick as close to **The One** who knows it all and acknowledge Him in all our ways. The transparent truth is that the tragedy of September 11th, 2001 was not a terrorist act but a self-inflicted wound carried out by rulers of the darkness of this world in high places in the United States. Please refer to Ephesians 6:12. "***For we do not wrestle against flesh and blood, but against principalities, against powers, against the rulers of the darkness of this age, against spiritual hosts of wickedness in the heavenly places.***"

God's ultimate concern for His steward is that His will is being carried out daily in their transformed lives. Therefore, we are to live a lifestyle reflective of Him as representatives of Heaven on earth because "…***you are the light of the world.***" Matthew 5:14. God wants us to know regardless of what happens, who it happens to or, when the unforeseen does occur, we will not perish eternally because we chose to stay in proper alignment with Him regardless of what we are facing! Throughout the upcoming chapters, I would like to point out, whenever you read the word "**HEART**," please apply it as follows:

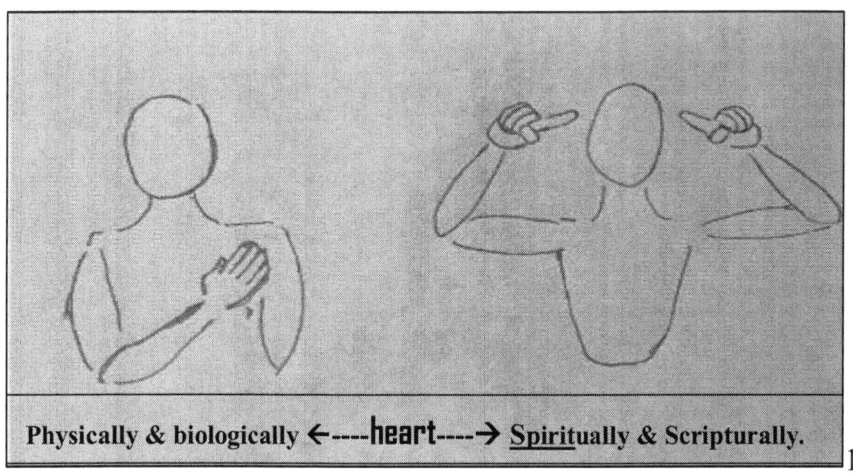

Physically & biologically ←----heart----→ Spiritually & Scripturally.[1]

Individual Review or Class Discussion

1—Please define **RE-PENT**. Also, the acronym.

2—What are some other ways **repent** is used today?

3—We know the word story is a fairy-tale or a real or imaginary account told for **entertainment**. In the **Word of Truth**, there are four other words mentioned which we can **substitute** for stories. They are:
1__________ 2. ____________ 3. __________ 4 .____________

4— Please write out the meaning in the acronym **COMMIT**?

C– **O**– **M**–
M– **I**– **T**–

5—In reading this work, would you categorize your current struggles as more **personal**, **spiritual** or **physical** in nature? Why?

6—Please complete Ephesians 6:12. "***We do not wrestle against flesh and***

7—Please complete the following verse about the Holy Spirit: "***In Him you also trusted, after you heard the word of truth, the gospel of your salvation; in whom also, having believed, you were*** ______

Eph. 1:13.

Chapter II-----------→ *Born Again*

Jesus' Introduction of the New Birth

It is critical to mention that the very first time '**born again**' was mentioned, it was by Jesus the Christ. When He did so, it was not aimed at students or laymen of the faith. Instead, it was directed to a religious ruler or teacher of that day named Nicodemus. ***See John 3:1-10***. Let us now carefully reexamine the encounter. We realize by Jesus disclosing spiritual truth to a theologian/teacher, everyone else should conclude if this "**born again**' model was a requirement for the teacher, it must also be required for the students as well.

Nicodemus, being a teacher of The Law, found it frustrating that he did not understand Jesus' teachings about God. This is the reason he sought to find Jesus late one night for the explanation of this 'new way,' governance and authority. In fact, it was Isaiah who saw what Messiah would be bringing to earth; "...***of the increase of His government and peace there shall be no end.***" Isaiah 9:6-7.

To paraphrase the late night inquiry, Nicodemus said to Jesus, all the other rulers *–Pharisees, high priests and religious leaders–*know you are truly a man sent from God. We talked among ourselves and concluded no one can do the wonders and miracles you do unless God is with them. But Rabbi, I still do not understand the things you say and do, even though I really believe I know about God as well. First, how do you do these miracles and by what authority do you do them? Secondly, why don't I *–a teacher of the Law–* understand these things?

Jesus' answer to Nicodemus' questions were very unique yet, they seemed so natural. Jesus pointed out that the element which prevented him from properly grasping spiritual understanding of the things he observed is the condition of his heart/mind. To put it another way, the same way no one can do these miracles except God is with them, it is the same way we cannot figure-out or perceive the things of The Awesome Kingdom of God unless a renewal in spirit takes place.

Without this re–birth you are spiritually **de**tached from God, but primarily in-tune to your five senses, their natural reasoning capabilities and the world around them. The Scripture points out, it is "***through faith we understand…***" Hebrews 11:3. Now let us further analyze and even reason deductively the encounter between Jesus and Nicodemus. If Jesus meant Nicodemus was entitled to this privilege of the new birth and it was **<u>not</u>** necessary for everyone else, He would be showing favoritism and being a respecter of persons which is sin. The scripture clearly states, " …***of a truth I perceive that God is no respecter of persons***." Acts 10:34.

Jesus gave Nicodemus the reason why he must be born a second time which is from above. "***Jesus answered and said unto him, Verily, verily, I say unto thee, except a man be born again, he cannot see the kingdom of God***." John 3:3. To put it a little differently, if being born again was not for everyone, then Jesus must have only wanted Nicodemus to acquire understanding of this supernatural unveiling which would allow him to enter into this kingdom exclusively.

By upholding this theory, it would **<u>exclude</u>** billions of people from potentially receiving the depth of understanding Nicodemus would have of God. Beloved, the rebirth is not for some but for everyone who wants to enter God's domain. God desires everyone to establish a closer relationship and a deeper understanding of Him, bar-none. Let us use a great acronym which details and explains exactly what **BORN–AGAIN** encompasses from God's vantage point:

B-irth
O-f
R-enewal *that's*
N-ecessary

A-llowing
G-rowth *to*
Accrue *by*
I-mplanting
N-ewness

Therefore, it is safe to conclude, the significance behind being born–again is to renew and implant newness by their Source who is God. God/**Adonai** means Lord/owner and His desire is that all humans be reconnected to Him/their Source through His Son's work. There is no other way to come to God! It is why Jesus said, ***"I Am The Way The Truth and The Life, no man comes to The Father but by Me"*** John 10:10**.** All who venture through this canal of the new birth will be able to understand God's written word for the **first time**.

As a special note, all things of God are spiritually perceived, not naturally picked-up. This new birth is mandatory for all so that no one can come to God by some other avenue or personal works. There never was or will ever be an exclusive invitation or secret code for any race, nationality, ethnicity, the rich, the poor, Asian, African, Indian, Caucasians, the scholar, the American, the foreigner to enter God's domain by their own way. Jesus said, "***I Am the Door***." John 10:9.

The Natural Birth and the Spiritual Birth

To be born naturally as we know it today, means there is a brand new life that has come into being which never existed before. Therefore, without birth there is no physical life. Both Peter in 1st Peter 1:23 and John in 1st John 1:9 specifically mentioned that without a rebirth, there will not emerge the change in our spirit which was designed to identify us with God. Rebirth brings us into the family of God through spiritual birth-right.

Throughout Jesus' ministry, He used natural every day common events and subjects such as birth, water, seed etc. to convey His points, so His messages could easily be understood. When Jesus mentioned birth, He was simply making a parallel between the physical birth – *we are familiar with*– and the new spiritual birth which brings about understanding of His administration. The spiritual or rebirth is intended to make our spirit conscious of the spiritual world. This is so that we get familiar with the other dimension in which God operates.

According to Jesus, we must be born into His realm spiritually just as we were born into the earthly realm physically. Let us ask a simple question. How did William of England become Prince? He was born prince through his lineage; no one made him Prince. Just as every human being has to be born through their earthly parents to come into this world physically, so everyone must experience this rebirth to reconnect to God spiritually. What a simple transition man complicated to cause confusion. When we mentioned Peter above, he stated, ***"having been born again, not of corruptible seed but incorruptible, through the word of God which lives and abides forever."*** 1 Peter 1:23. In reality, God's required new birth is not like its physical counterpart because; this one does not decay or become old.

Once this new birth has taken place *–by confessing and agreeing that Jesus is Lord–* we become a new resident in God's kingdom just as a baby becomes a new gift to their families in the physical realm. This is why the Scripture says, ***"Therefore, if anyone is in Christ, he is a new creation; old things have passed away; behold, all things have become new."*** 2 Corinthians 5:17. In the first Epistle of John, he mentions being "born of God" over five instances. There are also five (5) attributes associated with the new birth mentioned in his epistle. They are as follows:

1. It is a way to now **practice righteousness**; ***See I John 2:29***
2. Our spirit does not make **a common practice** to yield to sin. ***See I John 3:9***
3. This birth can allow us to now **love one another** sincerely and now our spirit **can know God**. ***See I John 4:7***
4. Our spirit can **become acquainted** with God through obedience because it is now birthed with the capacity to fulfill His propose. ***See I John 2:29***
5. We are now equipped to overcome hurdles. Hence the reason we are overcomers. ***See 1 John 5:4.***

The New Birth and the Kingdom of God

There are two vastly different perspectives surrounding the late-night meeting between Jesus and Nicodemus. Most people teach and arrive at the conclusion that the meeting was about how to be born again. However, this assumption is only from Nicodemus' perspective, not the premier subject Jesus was trying to convey. Jesus was speaking to him about entrance into the **K**ingdom of God, not about birth.

When my daughter was sixteen years old, I was speaking to her about the meeting between Nicodemus and Jesus. In the middle of unveiling this concealed mystery, she interrupted me and said, "I get it, I get it!" I mentioned to her that I was not finished explaining! Again, she boldly declared, "I get it, I get it!"

I looked at her and said, go ahead, tell me what you <u>think</u> you get! Actually, I was expecting her to say something inaccurate so I could correct her misunderstanding. However, this was not the case! The words which came out of this teenager were not only profound but filled with insight, clarity and revelation. She said the meeting was not about being born again, but how to get into the Kingdom of God. She went on to explain, 'I am here *–home–* and my school is over there *–eight miles away–* which is the destination; born again is the road I travel to get to my school which is to "The Kingdom!"

I was stunned and taken-back with this simple yet marvelous unveiling. Not only did she "steal my thunder" but it showed me God is still interested in our youths and He will continue to provide them with insight if they simply listen to what God will reveal to them. I mentioned to her, every time I teach this encounter to anyone, 'going forward' I will mention your detailed explanation.

Later, I mentioned to my wife *–as Jesus stated–* ***"out of the mouth of babes and suckling, thou has perfected praise."*** Matthew 21:16. I learned a great lesson about youths; God is still unveiling to them things we think we should be getting.

Rebirth and the Assigned Teacher

We are about to provide you with a multiple-choice question. "Please select the best answer which you think would allow you to personally acquire the best and most accurate understanding of God's Word."

A. "Howbeit when He, the Spirit of truth, is come, He will guide you into all truth..." **John 16:13**

B. "Study to show your-self approved unto God, a workman need not be ashamed rightly dividing the Word of truth." **2 Timothy 2:15**

C. "...searched the Scriptures daily to see if these things are so." **Acts 17:11**

D. "Be ready always to give an answer to every man that asks you a reason for the hope that is in you..." **I Peter 3:15.**

Even though all the above choices are relevant, true and scripturally sound, there is one which is critical for clarity and advancement; it is choice "A." The remaining three should be coordinated with the Holy Spirit. Choices B, C and D are personal pursuits for everyone.

On our own, if we studied, searched the Scriptures and were ready to provide answers to others, we would still need to be guided by the Holy Spirit on when, where and whom we are to share His message. Wouldn't you agree? In the past, all our involvement was in the natural region for all people living on earth.

Now that there are hundreds of religions to choose from, we need proper insight and discernment in order to come to the spiritually correct conclusions. It is why we have intentionally placed the following Scripture verse multiple times throughout this book. ***"But the natural man does not receive the things of the Spirit of God, for they are foolishness to him; nor can he know them, because they are spiritually discerned.*"** 1 Corinthians 2:14. We are to always opt for God's Holy Spirit in order to obtain spiritual truth.

Some people still have a tendency of holding on to what ministers teach. There are seminaries, Bible schools, colleges and study groups we attend to obtain insight. Others hold to the knowledge they acquired from college courses, jobs they have, employers, friends they have trusted, or parent's choice for their children. They have never sought the Holy Spirit for proper guidance and accurate information. Some of the above choices are meant to prepare us and may be good resources but we need unveiling from God's assigned teacher.

There is nothing wrong with obtaining historical studies about the Word of God. However, we are to obtain truth from the ultimate teacher who is the Holy Spirit. The Scripture warns, "***Beware lest any man spoil you through philosophy and vain deceit, after the tradition of men, after the rudiments of the world, and not after Christ.***" Colossians 2:8. The research and conclusions some have done or arrived at may be right for them but it may not be the course God has for *-you-* the ardent seeker. Always keep in mind, we were not only created to make a living, God made us and equipped each of us to "*...win souls*" *–Proverbs 11:30–* demonstrate a proper lifestyle and to make a difference in our generation. "*...**fear God, and keep his commandments: for this is the whole duty of man***." Eccl. 12:13.

Jesus said, "***Nevertheless I tell you the truth; It is expedient for you that I go away: for if I go not away, the Comforter will not come unto you; but if I depart, I will send him unto you.***" John 16:7. Some of the functions the Holy Spirit provides are to guide, remind, empower, abide and teach. Why, because we now represent the country of Heaven on earth as stewards and ambassadors. And, we need His instructions on how to effectively carry them out.

The Word of God says, "***This is the covenant that I will make with them after those days, says the LORD: I will put My laws into their hearts, and in their minds I will write them.***" Hebrews 10:16. The word 'heart' in Scripture is not that vessel in your chest which pumps blood. Whenever you read "heart/heart-of-man," it is referencing your sub-mind or subconscious mind. Please refer to the diagram on the bottom of page 13. This is the very core and consciousness of man.

Rebirth is for The Restoration of Leadership

With restoration on the forefront of God's plan for all His creation, let us start off this section with what most people perceive to be the weakest part of our composition. Yet, God sees it as the only place which is capable of containing His Holy Spirit. ***For my thoughts are not your thoughts, neither are your ways my ways, says the LORD*.**" Isaiah 55:8. God is letting us know we have to begin to change the way we think about Him from now on.

Before we confess Jesus as Lord, we know our **body** was king and number one in the pecking order because we constantly met its desires first. After all, it has always reigned supreme over the other two aspects of our being since our physical birth. Whenever or whatever sensual pleasures, hunger or desires the body craved, it invariably was granted and received immediate attention. The more we appeased the body, the more it craved. However, "***...do you not know that your body is the temple of the Holy Spirit who is in you, whom you have from God, and you are not your own? 20 For you were bought at a price; therefore, glorify God in your body and in your spirit, which are God's*.** I Cor. 6:18-20.

The part of our genetics which supports the body are the eyes; it provided the appeal of colors, shapes, sizes, desires and never got its fill of seeing. "...***the eye is not satisfied with seeing, nor the ear filled with hearing.***" Ecclesiastes 1:8. Next in line is our tongue which afforded the body the taste needed to indulge more-and-more. As much as our body was exposed to, it never received its fill but constantly craved even greater pleasures. Then, there are our ears which afforded us hearing from one another and music which made our body twist, turn, and move on its own. After all, the body has been the place where most of our experiences began and ended.

Next in line was our **soul**, which consists of our mind, our **desires** and our emotions; it is **not** mind, ~~will~~ and emotions which we will clarify later. The soul ran a close second to the body because it was responsible for everyday interacting and learning by experience. Our soul, in conjunction with our bodily senses seek to be socially accepted and coveted all the immediate things money could buy. As a result, God was placed on the back-burner as money became the primary motivator and multiple streams of income were sought. Pride was then birthed as another motivator as we wanted to exalt ourselves to shine in the limelight of friends, colleagues and associates.

Finally, there was our dormant **spirit.** As one could conclude from the self-indulgence of the body and soul *–listed above–* there was little room left for anything Godly. Our spirit was inactive since our natural physical birth surrounding the spiritual things of God. However, it was active for our function and existence as a human being. Remember, we are created in the image and likeness of our Source/Father God. It was Adam's transgression which severed us from our Source. As a result, our spirit yearns to be awakened from a state of stupor *–slumber–* to be reunited with its Creator God.

The 'rebirth of our spirit' provides the step *–like the refurbishing or a restoration of an old house, printer, car or equipment–* to its original state of its original design. The dormancy meant our spirit still existed, but it was not plugged into the ultimate power source. Therefore, it became a victim of neglect, its environment and misuse surrounded by elements and needed more attention. During this time, our body did permit our spirit temporary satisfaction of hearing the Word of God when we visited a church on a special occasion or someone ministered to us about salvation.

Other than a brief taste of spiritual matters, our spirit remained unplugged *–like an unused battery–* from God and subjected to the desires of its 'number one and two residents.' Based on the Word of God, we understand that the body could not be disciplined to effectively contain and administer God's plan unless the original order was restored. God's Word confirms by stating, ***"The spirit of man is the candle of the Lord searching all the inward parts of the belly."*** Proverbs 20:27. In other words, to those who are alive unto God through the rebirth, He sees a lit candle which gives light to their composition.

To the rest of the world who are without Christ, God sees them as a candle which needs to be rekindled. The spirit *–at times referred to as heart in the Old Testament–* constantly cries for the release of suffering from the bondage of slavery to the body's need/desires because our spirit was not created to follow, but to lead. The Scripture confirms, "…***because the creation itself also will be delivered from the bondage of corruption into the glorious liberty of the children of God.***" Romans 8:21. This yearning is what is prevalent in every human being regardless of nationality, religious affiliation or ethnicity. These include Buddhism, Catholicism, Judaism, Mormonism, Islam, Jehovah Witnesses, Christian, Atheist, Agnostic, Confucius, Scientology, or any other sect.

Almost everyone has chosen to associate themselves with a ceremonial form of worship or pursuit to find "God" because we hunger as spirit beings crying out to appease its nonphysical appetite. It is only through God's Word, we can read and observe the significance of the spirit, the composition of the soul, and the important role our body plays in God's overall plan.

Now we see why we are to diligently search/study God's Word. It has the right answers! The details are spelled out above how God intended us to function whenever someone decides to come to Christ. ***"And if Christ is in you, the body is dead because of sin, but the spirit is life because of righteousness."*** Romans 8:10. This can only be accomplished if we use the Word of God as our track to run on.

The Detailed Works of God's Holy Spirit

Whether someone recently confessed Jesus as Lord or feels they are a mature believer, God's awesome Holy Spirit reaches everyone at their present level of knowledge and personal situation. For example, in the Old Treaty, He reached saints with a still small voice. "***And after the earthquake a fire; but the LORD was not in the fire: and after the fire a still small voice.*** I Kings 19:12. However, in the New Treaty the Holy Spirit spoke audibly.

"***As they ministered to the Lord and fasted, the Holy Spirit said, "Now separate to Me Barnabas and Saul for the work to which I have called them.***" Acts 13:2. God's Word states, "***so, being sent out by the Holy Spirit.***" Acts 13:4. The association between the new birth and the rejoining of God's Holy Spirit to man's spirit means He ardently desires fellowship. We cannot have a spiritual union without spending quality time with God's Holy Spirit.

The Word of God then asks, "***What fruit did you have then in the things of which you are now ashamed? For the end of those things is death.***" Romans 6:21. This is because our old tendency to yield into sin is now being challenged because of the rekindling of our spirit to His Holy Spirit. Remember, the Scripture says, "***Therefore, if anyone is in Christ, he is a 'new creation;' old things have passed away; behold, all things have become new.***" II Corinthians 5:17. As a result of sin, most who call themselves believers confuse the feeling of **guilt** with a sense of **conviction**.

Guilt & Conviction; The By-Products of Sin

When someone confess Jesus as Lord, it is good to mention that even if they go back into sin, it will always yield a feeling of **guilt**, Guilt has a common applicable definition which we are all familiar with; it is to be held responsible for a boundary we crossed or something we did which our internal compass told us was not right. However, from our new understanding, guilt can be more accurately defined as a subjective conscious awareness that we internally know better. Remember the verse above, it states that we become a 'new creation!' Again, guilt carries a feeling of disappointment which is directed only to believers.

As a steward of God, our responsibility after an offense or sin has been committed is to run to our Father so the subjectivity of guilt does not keep us away from Him for any extended period of time. This is why the Scripture tells us, "***If we confess our sins, he is faithful and just to forgive us our sins, and to cleanse us from all unrighteousness***" I John 1:9. Wow, there can be restoration if we unintentionally sin. It is like when we put dirty clothes in a washing machine with detergent and turn it on. Beloved, when we choose to run to Our Father along with making a verbal confession what the actual sin is, we are cleansing ourselves. God does His part by putting us back on the track of righteousness. Our new outlook and desire should be to please our Father at all times and not to allow His Holy Spirit to become sad. "***And do not grieve*** –make sad– ***the Holy Spirit of God, by whom you were sealed for the day of redemption***." Eph. 4:30.

Guilt therefore, is not bad, neither is it from the enemy. When someone is born into the family of God, *–if they sin–* guilt can interfere with their thought processes which will change their approach towards God. Even in the natural, we only feel guilty when we know we have deliberately violated a trust, disappointed a parent, let down a friend or went away from someone who loves us. Isn't that true? Therefore, feeling guilty is a common feeling that sincere and conscientious people experience whenever they neglect to function or abide by God's standard.

There is an example in Scripture where it mentions people's conscience becoming insensitive to righteousness **"…*speaking lies in hypocrisy, having their own conscience seared with a hot iron.*"** I Timothy 4:2. This is where guilt can prevent us from seeking God. However, God wants to reconcile us so that we can be restored to Him and do better. Beloved, did you know, a non-believer feels very little guilt for any boundary they may cross? Why, because there was no prior solid commitment or road of loyalty they traveled.

Another by-product of sin is **<u>conviction</u>**. When we define conviction today, we know it as the act or process of finding or proven guilty. However, God's definition of conviction and the means by which it applies to a believer takes on a whole new direction. This is because it does not involve guilt or having to live with a guilty conscience. Jesus said, **"*And when He*** – *the Holy Spirit–* ***is come, He will reprove*** *–convict–* ***the world of sin, of righteousness, and of judgment*:"** John 16:8.

We hope it is clear that the Holy Spirit convicts the world as well as believers. However, being convicted does not mean we are sentenced for execution or punishment. This prompting by the Holy Spirit will put us on high alert that we are ignoring something which can cause separation. **"*For as many as are led by the Spirit of God, they are the***

sons of God. " Romans 8:14. From now on, no one has to tell us what we do, or what we are about to do is wrong because we will know it internally. God dwells within us individually but also collectively as the body in Christ. The Scripture confirms, "…***We are all one in Christ.*** " Galatians 3:28. No one is above another, no matter what earthly title they have achieved to put behind their name! The Holy Spirit is limitless in His administration. However, He is **only** limited by what we choose to **ex**clude from Him.

If we constantly yield to the pleasures of sin, He becomes sad. God's Holy Spirit will not just direct us into spiritual things, but also in our interactions with friends, family, relationships, decisions on the job, and even daily recreational activities. Conviction is designed to keep us on track. Therefore, from this day forward, always *–petition–* your Father in the name of Jesus before reading or studying His Manual. This is so that His Holy Spirit can provide greater insight and broader outlook of revelation into God's Word. There is a very common word which we used earlier to describe the works of the Holy Spirit in our daily lives. It was the word **GREAT**. He can:

G uide you into **all** truth……………………………………John 16:13
R emind you of **all** things………………………………….John 14:26
E mpower you to act on earth on Heaven's behalf…………Acts 1:8
A bide in you because you are God's temple on earth……I Cor. 6:18
T each you **all** things as a believer in Christ………………John 14:26

By simply acknowledging God's Holy Spirit in all we do, He will be able to provide greater insight, early warning and instruct us to take a different route/approach. Then, He wants our lifestyle to shine as a beacon of light to the world so God gets all the glory. "***Let your light so shine before men, that they may see your good works, and glorify your Father which is in Heaven.*** " Matthew 5:16.

Throughout this book, we have deliberately mentioned this particular verse numerous times. Remember, all kinds of problems will await us to try and redirect us from God's standards. The Scripture unveils to us, "***Many are the afflictions of the righteous: but the LORD delivers him out of them all.*** " Psalms 34:19. As a concerned Father, God wants us to be guilt free and "***be ready always to give an answer to every man that asks you a reason for the hope that is in you***…"

I Peter 3:15. Your Father who is also God, loves you and wants you to succeed, prosper and provide answers so that you bring others aboard.

Individual Review or Class Discussion

1—Please complete the verse; "***Therefore if anyone be in Christ He is a new***
____

______________________________________ ***2 Cor.5:17***

2—The Word of God says, "***Many are the afflictions of the***______ ***but the LORD***
____

______________________________________ Ps. 34:19

3—***Being 'born again' not of corruptible*** _____________***but by the***
____

____

______________________________________ I Pet. 1.23

4—The meeting between **Jesus** and Nicodemus was primarily about:
____

____

5--Please fill-in the acronym **BORN AGAIN**?
____

B–	**A–**
O–	**G–**
R–	**A–**
N–	**I–**
	N–

6—Born again only pertains to this part of your composition**,** it is our…
____

7—Please complete the difference between **guilt** and **conviction.**
Guilt is ___________________Conviction is___________________

____

Chapter III----------→ *Saved*

For those who are newly born into the family of God by their confession of Jesus as Lord, this section will be like a covert operation filled with detailed insight. It involves God's plan which has been strategically thought out and arranged before the foundations of the world; it has been in place and always accessible so that anyone can participate. The Scriptures support this statement. ***"Just as He chose us in Him before the foundation of the world, that we should be holy and without blame before Him in love, having predestined us to adoption as sons by Jesus Christ to Himself, according to the good pleasure of His will."*** Ephesians 1:4-5.

This strategy was meticulously prepared just so believers could begin to see how God's plan of salvation fits into their new lives. However, some may not have a clear understanding of who they really are or, His process; hence the reason for an ungodly lifestyle. The minister or friend who has been praying for their salvation makes up a part of this specialized unit. Let us refer to this plan as "Operation Head-Start." Let us start with the word **SAVE** from God's vantage point. It points out that:

S-alvation
A-ffords *a*
V-iew *of*
E-ternity

God created mankind to live forever. However, the world view has painted a picture of life as being personal and individualistic. There are ways in which people will perceive God and His Word to be; then, there are His principles in which He requires us to practice and follow. God's Word provides us with support by His Holy Spirit who teaches us truth and extends to all God's plan of salvation.

"But the anointing which you have received from Him abides in you, and you do not need that anyone teach you; but as the same anointing teaches you concerning all things, and is true, and is not a lie, and just as it has taught you, you will abide in Him." 1 John 2:27. You may hear or have heard the old excuse that man wrote the

Bible/Word of God. This can't be true because God's Word points out, "***For prophecy never came by the will of man, but holy men of God spoke as they were moved by the Holy Spirit.***" II Peter 1:21. Furthermore, the Scripture says, "***But the natural man does not receive the things of the Spirit of God, for they are foolishness to him; nor can he know them, because they are spiritually discerned.***" 1 Corinthians 2:14.

More time and emphasis is devoted to this section because '**save**' is not only the most common of the four terms used when pointing out salvation, it is also the most misunderstood. The implementation of His operation and the unveiling of His plans will provide us with a bird's eye view of God's unique process. Therefore, from His unveiling, salvation should no longer be seen as a jigsaw puzzle but a finished picture showing His endless brilliance.

What Does It Mean to Be Saved?

To be saved pertains to the part of our composition *–the soul–* which has to be rescued from the path of certain destruction to the light of God's Word. The Word says that it is God, "***who desires all men to be saved and to come to the knowledge of the truth.***" I Timothy 2:4. Please notice the detailed sequence. Our soul must first be rescued and redirected from the course of error *–saved–* in order to gain proper knowledge of God's Word. You may have heard someone say, 'I am saved', and probably the first question which came to mind was, 'saved from what?' Basically, the word '**save**' means to rescue or deliver as pertaining to a person.

In order for someone to be rescued, they must have been off course or lost. And, in order for there to be a rescue, provisions had to be made so that they could be delivered from the place of exile back to familiar territory. Jesus is the vehicle God used to transport all humans back to their rightful status. This is why He *-Jesus-* is called our Savior of the world. "***And we have seen and do testify that the Father sent the Son to be the Savior of the world.***" 1 John 4:14. This means provision has to be made by someone other than the person who is lost. It also means man could not save himself. "***For our conversation is in heaven; from whence also we look for the Savior, the Lord Jesus Christ.***"

Philippians 3:20. As we know, in order for the word rescue to apply, one's own effort cannot be part of the equation. In other words, if we can rescue ourselves, we do not need God's provision. Through no initial personal fault of our own, mankind was separated from God because of Adam. "***For as by one man's disobedience many were made sinners...***" Romans 5:19. He was the one who brought about this separation of human beings from the Source –who is God– through his transgression.

The familiar territory is the restoration to a high status with our Father who is in Heaven. ***"And hath raised us up together, and made us sit together in heavenly places in Christ Jesus.***" Ephesians 2:6. The reality is everyone born physically into this world today is at enmity with God. "***For to be carnally minded is death, but to be spiritually minded is life and peace. Because the carnal mind is enmity against God; for it is not subject to the law of God, nor indeed can be."*** Romans 8;6-7.

All humans are lost in their direction without God's divine intervention. As a result, man has to be delivered from the path of self-righteousness and being too physically conscious, which blocks their ability to pick-up God. Today, whenever someone reads or hears the word '*saved*' concerning salvation, it is directed only to their soul and not to the spirit or body. As a result, when someone says, *'I am saved'*, they are saying my soul *–which involves the mind, the <u>desires</u> and the emotions–* has now been **re**introduced to God and His living Word which provided the track to run-on back to Him.

Only God's provision *–Jesus Christ–* can make this destination a true reality. The Word confirms, "***Neither is there salvation in any other, for there is no other name under heaven given among men by which we must be saved.***" Acts 4:12. An easily identifiable system of salvation is like having a parachute on a plane. You would <u>**not**</u> jump out of an airplane without having one on but trust in the parachute –***<u>Jesus</u>***– to provide you with protection, security which will ensure a safe landing.

What Does God's Plan of Salvation Entail?

The whole scope of salvation is for our **spirit** to be reborn in order to restore the proper order to our composition. Initially, when we confess Jesus as Lord, the major change which occurred is that God's Holy Spirit came to join our spirit and seal us. Again, "…***in whom also after that you believed, you were sealed with that holy Spirit of promise***." Ephesians 1:13. Next, our **soul** *–mind–* is being fed new nourishment and information so we could grasp His new principles as He originally intended. Finally, our temporary house –**the body**– can become the dwelling–place of His Holy Spirit.

The Word wakes us up by asking, "***what, do you not know that your body is the temple of the Holy Spirit who is in you, whom you have from God, and you are not your own? For you were bought at a price; therefore, glorify God in your body and in your spirit, which are God's.***" I Corinthians 6:19-20. Jesus said, we are to let our light and lifestyle be displayed so vividly that the world sees a clear distinction. "***let your light so shine before men that they may see your good works and glorify your father which is in Heaven***." Matthew 5:16. What an awesome statement! We have to realize that we are always being observed, even when we think no one is watching.

Now we can vividly see that the conversion process involves the understanding of a change which takes place spiritually. And, there is new information transmitted mentally. As a result, our body becomes the temple of God and His Holy Spirit physically. We are to embrace the fact that we are no longer our own *–as stated above–* according to Scripture.

As offspring, God has constructed us in a way whereby our soul *–mind–* cannot be delivered from the course of adverse knowledge unless our spirit is born again. And, our natural mind cannot properly grasp His Spiritual Truth unless it is submitted to His directives. Neither can our spirit be born of God unless we believe and confess Jesus Christ is Lord of our new life in God. This is not a new doctrine, sect or religious belief, but the reality of what God's Word has clearly spelled out about salvation for all mankind in great detail.

Great Details about the Soul of Man

There is the real 'you' God is concerned about which is your most valuable asset to Him. "***For what profit is it to a man if he gains the whole world, and loses his <u>own soul</u>? Or what will a man give in exchange for <u>his soul</u>***?" Matthew 16:26. According to Jesus' description, man's most valuable asset to God is their soul. Evidence of which was spelled out when Jesus detailed the encounter between a rich man and Lazarus who both died and He proceeded to express exactly what took place immediately afterwards.

19 There was a certain rich man, which was clothed in purple and fine linen, and fared sumptuously every day:

20 And there was a certain beggar named Lazarus, which was laid at his gate, full of sores,

21 And desiring to be fed with the crumbs which fell from the rich man's table: moreover, the dogs came and licked his sores.

22 And it came to pass, that the beggar died, and was carried by the angels into Abraham's bosom: the rich man also died, and was buried;

23 And in hell he lifted up his eyes, being in torments, and seeing Abraham afar off, and Lazarus in his bosom.

24 And he cried and said, Father Abraham, have mercy on me, and send Lazarus that he may dip the tip of his finger in water, and cool my tongue; for I am tormented in this flame.

25 But Abraham said, Son, remember that thou in thy lifetime received thy good things, and likewise Lazarus evil things: but now he is comforted, and thou art tormented.

26 And beside all this, between us and you there is a great gulf fixed: so that they which would pass from hence to you cannot; neither can they pass to us, that would come from thence.

27 Then he said, I pray thee therefore, father, that you would send him to my father's house:

28 For I have five brethren; that he may testify unto them, lest they also come into this place of torment.

29 Abraham said unto him, they have Moses and the prophets; let them hear them.

30 And he said, Nay, father Abraham: but if one went unto them from the dead, they will repent.

31 And he said unto him, if they hear not Moses and the prophets, neither will they be persuaded, though one rose from the dead". Luke 16:19-31.

Let us now examine this afterlife encounter carefully. Jesus said there was a particular man and a particular beggar; the beggar even had a particular name, Lazarus. No one gives a teaching –not ~~story~~– and uses a name unless it is true and relevant. After they both died physically in verse twenty-two, a real description and conversation began to unfold. We can now see the big picture in plain sight.

Therefore, this parable was not an illustration, but it paralleled the facts about two men who lived in the same country physically, yet they were separated after physical death. One was righteous and served God; the other unrighteous and enjoyed life without acknowledging God who gave him those things to enjoy including the pleasure of life. This account took place before Jesus' resurrection.

Again, notice the rich man and Lazarus both died and their bodies were carried away to be buried physically in **verse 22**. Take note also of both their consciousness and present mental faculties to recognize *–without physical eyes–* where they were and even distinguish their circumstance **without** their body being present in **verses 23-24**. Remember, our soul consists of our **mind** *–to recall, reason and discern–* which is demonstrated in **verse 24**. Then, there are de**sires** expressed in detail about his situation. He knew where he was but he was not able to choose but desired to change his circumstance. Did you notice in verse thirty (30) that the rich man made an urgent request/appeal? Finally, there is his human **emotion** which is an intense mental activity triggered by how someone feels. As we know, feelings are not always rational in decision-making which you will observe a little later. However, in this case, the rich man's desires and concerns are expressed towards his physical living relatives who are not with him; **verse 28**. This is why he said, "***For I have five brothers, that he may testify to them, lest they also come to this place of torment."*** We see, if it was possible, the rich man would like a second chance to warn his family members to make a wise choice. Again, he realizes a decision must be made while he's alive physically. If not, he knew their soul would come to this place where he is which is not where he wanted his family members to end up.

The supporting Scripture says, "***And as it is appointed unto men once to die, but after this the judgment***," Hebrews 9:27. God wants us not only to read but to inwardly absorb His truth which is again in plain sight. Remember, revelation is not just the unveiling of something previously unknown. It is a higher exposure to God's Word which we have read, believed or employed. Then, it can take on a deeper understanding based on a close communion with God's Holy Spirit.

The Word says, "...***how that by revelation He made known to me the mystery (as I have briefly written already, by which, when you read, you may understand my knowledge in the mystery of Christ), which in other ages was not made known to the sons of men, as it has now been revealed by the Spirit to His holy apostles and prophets***." Ephesians 3:3-5.

The Soul of Man Prior & After Jesus' Resurrection

In reviewing the creation of man, God said, man *–the specie–* became something after the body was made and the spirit was breathed into it. God said, "...***man became a living soul***" Genesis 2:7. Notice, God did not say the man became a living body even though it was formed out of something physical. Neither does it say the man became a living spirit, despite the very *'breath of life'* which came out from God

Himself to give the *–dust/water–* clay figure life. Our Heavenly Father made a part of us *–the house from dirt–* and created a part of us *–spirit–* from Himself yet, God sees man's essential characteristic as primarily a living entity which He calls the '**soul**.'

The God-Head –not trinity– written only three (3) times –Colossians 3:9, Acts 17:29 and Romans 1:20– consists of Father, Son and Holy Spirit, ***"For there are three that bear witness in heaven: The Father, the Word, and the Holy Spirit; and these three are one."*** 1 John 5:7.***"*** The word trinity is not wrong; it is just not Scriptural especially when ministering to other religious groups. **Godhead** is irrefutable. Again, the only Biblically correct word for the Father, Son and Holy Spirit is Godhead! When ministering to others, let us use what is written, not what man has theorized or made up.

Beloved, every human-being comprises of a **spirit** being, which possesses a **soul** and lives in a physical house or body. We are also three distinct entities manifested in one physical construction on earth. We are also a three distinct entities manifested in one physical construction on earth. "***Now may the God of peace Himself sanctify you completely; and may your whole spirit, soul, and body be preserved blameless at the coming of our Lord Jesus Christ***." I Thessalonians 5:23. Just as the Godhead functions in unison and harmony, so man's composition was originally constructed by God to function harmoniously until Adam's original sin changed the order and was brought upon all humans.

After Jesus' physical death and physical bodily resurrection –***and He did eat before them***" Luke 24:43– He provided the gateway for all who died since Abel *–Adam's second oldest son–* to enter Heaven. It is important to note that all the saints who ever lived and died before Jesus' physical appearance, their souls did not go to Heaven but were held in a place called Abraham Bosom. Luke 16:22**.** Conversely, those who did not serve God, their souls went to a place called Hades –this was a holding area– prior to His resurrection. As we know, after Jesus' resurrection; the Old Testament saints were resurrected *–came to life again–* to walk with Jesus on earth and appeared unto many before He led them to Heaven. "***And coming out of the graves after His***

resurrection, they went into the holy city and appeared to many*.**" Matthew 27:53. The Apostle Paul shed further light on this profound truth and new transition when he spoke about Jesus, "...When He ascended on high, He led captivity captive*** –free–, ***and gave gifts to men. Now this, "He ascended" what does it mean but that He also <u>first</u> descended into the lower parts of the earth?*** Ephesians 4:8-9.

According to some Bible Scholars, the two exceptions are Enoch and Elijah *–who never died–* and are currently in Heaven today. The devil once had the keys and power of death. "***Inasmuch then as the children have partaken of flesh and blood, He Himself likewise shared in the same, that through death He might destroy him who had the power of death, that is, the devil*.**" Hebrews 2:14, Jesus' descent was to take back the keys, release the souls of those who were in captivity *–custody–* and provide the passage-way for the Old Testament saints to enter Heaven.

You see saint, what Jesus accomplished after His death while on earth provides believers with permanency and the access into Heaven when death occurs. Through Jesus' work then, when a believer dies now, both their soul and spirit are immediately transported to be present with the Lord. Now we can understand why The Scripture states, "***We are confident, yes, well pleased rather to be <u>absent from the body</u> and to be <u>present with the Lord</u>*.**" 2 Corinthians 5:8. You see saint of God, Jesus made the way so the most valuable part of man *–the soul, the real you–* can reside with God forever. What a great transitional work Jesus did within a short three-day span.

Is Labor (Work) Required in Obtaining Salvation?

One of the most common misconceptions associated with obtaining salvation is that good works (*labor*) is necessary in order to secure it. The idea that we have to perform some work or function stems from misunderstanding of the following Scripture. "***Therefore, my beloved, as you have always obeyed, not as in my presence only, but now much more in my absence, <u>work out your own salvation with fear</u>***

and trembling." Philippines 2:12. When the Scripture says, "*work out your own salvation*" it does not mean to engage in physical or mental activities so you can obtain a status for your own efforts. Instead, it means to accomplish or complete God's plan for your life by agreeing and confessing Jesus as Lord. The only work required is a confession and belief which the Word of God confirms. "***For by grace you have been saved through faith, and that not of yourselves; it is the gift of God,*** [9] ***not of works, lest anyone should boast.***" Ephesians 2:8. As humans, we like to take credit for what we do. However, salvation is an undeserved favor provided for mankind by God through the sacrificial death of His son Jesus.

"***For God so loved the world that He gave His only begotten Son, that whoever believes in Him should not perish but have everlasting life***." John 3:16. In the Old Treaty, it was the blood of animals which was used for the annual covering/atonement for the sins of the people. However, God provided the ultimate sacrifice –*His* ***only*** *begotten son*– and as a result, the New Treaty became the permanent solution.

Our New Covenant says, "***not by works of righteousness which we have done, but according to His mercy He saved us, through the washing of regeneration and renewing of the Holy Spirit, whom He poured out on us abundantly through Jesus Christ our Savior.***" Titus 3:5-6. Washing denotes a necessary cleansing; rebirth involves a required step. And, refurbishing is a renovation process carried out by the Holy Spirit. Beloved, as you have noticed, both grace and mercy are mentioned. The difference is, grace is getting something you don't deserve; mercy is not getting what you **do** deserve.

- *How is our soul* –saved– *delivered from the path of separation from God?* This work is accomplished through the washing of rebirth of our spirit.
- *Whose responsibility or function is it to see cleansing and redirection takes place once belief is initiated?* This job is reserved exclusively for His Holy Spirit.

- *<u>How is our spirit reborn?</u>* It is by the reintroduction *–renewal–* of God's precious Holy Spirit to our own which is initiated by our confession that "**<u>Jesus is Lord</u>**."

Therefore, salvation is not something anyone can personally work for or achieve by effort because the work to redeem man back to God has already been paved. There was an innocent life which was taken for the entire world's sin. This is why the Scripture says we are God's purchased possession. "***Therefore, take heed to yourselves and to all the flock, among which the Holy Spirit has made you overseers, to shepherd the church of God which He purchased with His own blood***. Acts 20:28. Is this verse telling us that <u>God</u> has <u>blood</u>? Yes, through His only begotten son! Salvation is now a free undeserved gift provided by God for all mankind. Again, all that is required is our confession and belief of God's only begotten son.

I love God; He is way smarter than we are! Now let us be very honest with ourselves. If it was possible for you to do some work or labor to obtain eternal life on your own and you worked the hardest, wouldn't you feel if you were to slip-up, come-up short somehow or sin, you should deserve more of a second or third chance? Beloved, it would not be fair if someone could work for salvation. Why, because some people are physically <u>stronger</u>, mentally more <u>perceptive</u>, socially more <u>articulate</u>, and economically <u>wealthier</u> than others.

This would make it easy for some to obtain and extremely difficult or impossible for others to get if any of the foregoing was the standard requirement. Age would also play a significant factor. Therefore, if salvation could be bought, only the rich would be able to afford it. And, if it was based on how much education one has achieved, only the scholars would understand. Throughout the Scriptures, God has clearly spelled out that His ways are not our ways.

Having God to provide the standard *–who is no respecter of persons–* all would be equal and on a level playing field. "***Then Peter opened his mouth, and said, of a truth I perceive that God is no respecter of persons.***" Acts 10:34. This means God does NOT favor one race or nation of people above another because ***"there is neither Jew nor***

Greek, there is neither slave nor free, there is neither male nor female; for you are all one in Christ Jesus." Galatians 3:28. Finally, "***and He has made from <u>one blood</u> every nation of men to dwell on all the face of the earth***..." Acts 17:26. Because of who God is, everyone starts out on an equal plateau being given the same measure of faith to begin with and to build on. **Isn't God great and marvelous!** In Paul's second letter to Timothy, the Scriptures clearly states, God "...***who has saved us and called us with a holy calling, not according to our works, but according to His own purpose and grace which was given to us in Christ Jesus before time began***." II Timothy 1:9. "***Even when we were dead in sins has made us alive together with Christ, by grace ye are saved***." Eph. 2:5.

The Great Value & Treasure of Our Thought Life

Let us start out by asking you one of the most important questions of all surrounding your relationship with God. From the choices below, please select the **<u>one</u>** you think is your **<u>most valuable asset</u>** in your daily communion with Him. If you do not see your choice below, please place it on the blank #7 space provided. The choices are:

1. Loving God and loving one another genuinely
2. Reading/studying and meditating on His Word
3. Faith, worshipping and praising God
4. Ministering the Good News to others and saving souls
5. Forgiving one another; returning tithe and offerings
6. Praying for others including prayer and fasting
7. ______________________________

As imperative as all the above requirements are to carry out in our relationship with God, the most critical one is **<u>not</u>** listed. The one which God values most is 'our thought life.' All of the above comes in a distant second. The Word of God clearly confirms that our thought life is primary and it is spelled out in His Library's Collection.

1. ***For as a man <u>thinks</u> in his heart, so he is."*** ....**Proverbs 23:7**
2. Be **<u>transformed</u>** by the **<u>renewing</u>** of your **<u>mind</u>**,.......**Rom. 12:1-2**
3. Jesus stated, why do **<u>thoughts</u>** arise.....................**Luke 24:38**
4. God will keep us in perfect peace whose **<u>mind</u>**.........**Isaiah 26:3**

5. Where does **repent** begin; what does it mean?................**Acts 2:38**
6. The **thought** of foolishness is sin............................**Prov.24:9**
7."Out of the abundance of the **heart...**" *–mind–*............**Luke 6:45**
8."Casting down imaginations and...thoughts...............**II Cor. 10:5**

At the pinnacle of our relationship with God stands **our thought life**. This is the primary key and our most vital quality which God honors greatly in all of His offspring. Simeon was the first person in the New Testament to point out that Jesus was coming primarily to address the thoughts of man. "*...that the **thoughts of many hearts** may be **revealed***." Luke 2:35. Please refer to the diagram on the bottom of page 13. In essence, it is the things we think in our subconscious minds that matters **most** to God.

In order for us to maintain a genuine working relationship with Our Lord, He stated what we are to do in the (#8) example on the previous page. What God hates is, "***a mind that devises wicked imaginations***" Prov. 6:17-19. Now let us spell out #8 completely. It states, "***Casting down imaginations, and every high thing that exalts itself against the knowledge of God and bringing into captivity every thought to the obedience of Christ.***" II Corinthians 10:5-6. We are to cast down contrary imaginations because it interferes with our relationship!

Why would it be so imperative to flush our opposing thoughts down the toilet? This is because our thoughts are first to arrive on the scene before any actions are taken or results manifested. Why do you think when we see or hear of someone who has done something outlandish or strange, our first **thought** is usually, "what were they **thinking**?"

Let us now point out another major difference between the Treaties.

Old Testament	**New Testament**
1-Sexual act was adultery----	**look w/engaging thought = adultery**
2-Murder was taking a life---	**If we hate someone; this = murder**

Now let us disclose the primary reason why God destroyed the cities of Sodom and Gomorrah? Was it a result of what they did, what they were doing or, was it their perversion? The Word of God clearly spells out the reason. "***And GOD saw that the wickedness of man was great***

in the earth, and that every <u>imagination of the thoughts</u> of his heart –subconscious mind– ***was only evil continually***." Genesis 6:5.

This is why God's Manual says we are to discard vain imaginations and contrary thoughts because they are our number-one hindrance. The things others perceive about us stems first from their thoughts. The way a person thinks can halt, hinder or permanently sever their relationship with God. Man, *–the specie–* brought separation on themselves through the avenue of their thought life which is always first to step out of bounds. Our soul *-brain function-* has the capability to effectively guide us by using the new knowledge it has gained in God's Word to identify and separate our dos from our don'ts. This is why our soul becomes the enemy's primary target.

Our Thoughts/Mind and the enemy

Contrary to what most people have heard about the works of the enemy, some still believe he and his demons can put thoughts in our mind. The enemy **<u>CANNOT</u>** put thoughts in the mind of any true believer. Case and point! ***Therefore, if any man be in Christ, he is a new creature: old things are passed away; behold, all things are become new***." II Corinthians 5:17. You cannot be a renewed believer and the enemy has 24/7 access to your mind because "…***we have the mind of Christ***." I Corinthians 2:16. The Lord and the devil can NEVER inhabit the same space, temple or body; it is **IMPOSSIBLE**!

Some people might immediately default to the devil's influence of Judas who betrayed Jesus; this is a good argument but a weak case based on the evidence. Let us reveal how the enemy entered Judas. Despite the fact that God walked with Judas every day, his subconscious mind was not in the right place or properly aligned. Judas was a thief from the beginning who valued/loved money. It was the love of money that corrupted him which provided the enemy the avenue and appeal to his greed and personal innate desire.

"***For the love of money is a root of all kinds of evil, for which some have strayed from the faith in their greediness, and pierced themselves through with many sorrows***." I Timothy 6:10. You see beloved, despite God working miracles through Judas, He will NOT change what is really in anyone unless they ask, they are sincere and desire to change. The Word tells us, "...***but all things are naked and open to the eyes of Him to whom we must give account***." Hebrews 4:13. Let us ask this qualifying and detailed question; who was Judas more focused on, God or his greed for cash? Do you know, there are some believers today who claim to know God and God does NOT know them? Jesus specifically told us, "***Many will say to Me in that day, 'Lord, Lord, have we not prophesied in Your name, cast out demons in Your name, and done many wonders in Your name?' And then I will declare to them, 'I never knew you; depart from Me, you who practice iniquity***." Matthew 7:22-23.

People of various denominations read this verse without ever focusing or desiring to analyze the significance of the last word Jesus mentioned which we underlined; it is **iniquity**. In other words, some believers have one foot in the world and the other in the church. These deviations include sexual intimacy outside of marriage, jealousy, prejudice, hatred, envy, pride evil desires and evil thoughts toward others. The people who embrace and engage in these things are setting themselves up for failure. They do not realize they are traveling in the same boat as Judas which is only a matter of time before they sink.

Remember, Jesus said "***no one can serve two masters; for either he will hate the one and love the other, or else he will be loyal to the one and despise the other. You cannot serve God and*** –money– ***mammon***." Matthew 6:24. Again, who was Judas more focused on, God or his greed for cash? It is only when we choose to open the door that the enemy and his cohorts can implant thoughts due to access we provide. According to Scripture, these are the facts; let no one tell you something different!

We are about to disclose other ways our adversary can have place in us; it is only **IF** they play with a Ouija Board, practice witchcraft, play or played dungeons and dragons or engage in Tarot card reading, horoscope or other demonic/satanic practice(s). The Word of God points out, "***give no place to the devil***." Ephesians 4:27. If we do not give him access, he cannot act!

Therefore, we CANNOT practice sorcery/evil and have God at the same time. Spiritual laws must always be violated or we would not be able to trust God. If you are a parent or guardian of the innocent, do you bring bad things on your child or children or, do they bring things on themselves through disobedience? As you are aware, God relates His people to sheep which is not exactly a compliment. Did you know sheep follow each other despite adverse situations? Also, did you know if there is a cliff and the sheep ahead falls off to its death, the others will follow to the same demise?

Throughout God's Word, He provides us with very easy questions followed by very easy/obvious answers immediately following. This is so that we do **NOT** even have to ponder. He said, "***I call heaven and earth as witnesses today against you, that I have set before you life and death, blessing and cursing; therefore choose life, that both you and your descendants may live***." Deuteronomy 30:19. As you can see, the choices we make today will impact us and our descendants.

During my one-on-one or in Bible study sessions when Matthew 7:22-23 arises, almost everyone defaults to the "no relationship with God theory." Over the past ten years, I have not met anyone who mentioned iniquity as the root cause! Even those who minister door-to-door have escalated this particular verse to an extreme level; they use it as the reason for **not** praying for others. The key word in this verse is iniquity which is a secret transgression. Again, the 'no' **relationship** with Him notion is not accurate or true. The Scripture specifically outlines that:

1st..They called Jesus 'Lord/Owner.'
2nd...They proclaimed Him where ever they went.
3rd..They cast out demons by delegated authority! See **Luke 10:19**
4th..Finally, they did wonderful works in **His name!** How could you do these works and not have a relationship with Him? **IMPOSSIBLE**!

Beloved, these people Jesus mentioned had a relationship and was even empowered by His Holy Spirit but they had hidden/covert and ungodly secrets going-on behind closed doors. This is like some pastors and ministers today. They have girlfriends, boyfriends they sleep with; they follow the yellow-brick road of non-ending stream of cash-flow, watch pornography, engage in adverse lifestyle, some do illegal drugs and alcohol etc. Even the old folks knew better! Simon, for example, was a magician in Samaria who bewitched the people with all kinds of drugs and evil influence. And, he was a sorcerer but knew internally that he could not have God and still practice evil.

9 "But there was a certain man called Simon, who previously practiced sorcery in the city and astonished the people of Samaria, claiming that he was someone great,

10 To whom they all gave heed, from the least to the greatest, saying, "This man is the great power of God."

11 And they heeded him because he had astonished them with his sorceries for a long time.

12 But when they believed Philip as he preached the things concerning the kingdom of God and the name of Jesus Christ, both men and women were baptized.

13 Then Simon himself also believed; and when he was baptized he continued with Philip, and was amazed, seeing the miracles and signs which were done.

14 Now when the apostles who were at Jerusalem heard that Samaria had received the word of God, they sent Peter and John to them,

15 who, when they had come down, prayed for them that they might receive the Holy Spirit.

16 For as yet He had fallen upon none of them. They had only been baptized in the name of the Lord Jesus.

17 Then they laid hands on them, and they received the Holy Spirit.

18 And when Simon saw that through the laying on of the apostles' hands the Holy Spirit was given, he offered them money,

19 saying, "Give me this power also, that anyone on whom I lay hands may receive the Holy Spirit."

20 But Peter said to him, "Your money perish with you, because you thought that the gift of God could be purchased with money!

21 "You have neither part nor portion in this matter, for your heart is not right in the sight of God.

22 "Repent therefore of this your wickedness, and pray God if perhaps the thought of your heart may be forgiven you.

23 "For I see that you are poisoned by bitterness and bound by iniquity."

24 Then Simon answered and said, "Pray to the Lord for me, that none of the things which you have spoken may come upon me."

25 ***So when they had testified and preached the word of the Lord, they returned to Jerusalem, preaching the gospel in many villages of the Samaritans***." Acts 8:9-25. As painful as it is to mention, our ancestor's involvement in the occult and secret transgression – *iniquity*– are the main players in this major league of possession, influence, sickness and degenerative disease. What we are attempting to treat with drugs, surgery and meditation God spells out as evil which we need to pray and fast over in order to obliterate it! We or our ancestors must violate/**embrace** some spiritual law(s) in order for the enemy to inflict us; remember, our enemy is **always** governed by laws because he's **NOT** God!

God has given us deputized authority to break any curse, strongholds and spells in **Jesus** name! Again, our enemy's primary plan is to try and appeal to our own greed/desires through our own lust of the flesh, lust of our eyes and for us to defend our personal pride. Our pride, words and chosen lifestyle will unlock the front door of our mind for him (the enemy) to enter and take-up residence. "***Then he goes and takes with him seven other spirits more wicked than himself, and they enter and dwell there; and the last state of that man is worse than the first.***" Luke 11:26.

Once we unlock the door of our minds to ungodly activities, he can come to visit every other room of our soul and bring other spirits to take up residence indefinitely. Then, he can legally stay and influence our thoughts, life and generations to come. Please note, we have the authority to lock him out by verbalizing our situation to Our Father in Jesus' name. "***And I will give you the keys of the kingdom of heaven, and whatever you bind*** –lock up– ***on earth will be bound in heaven,***

and whatever you loose –allow or permit–***on earth will be loosed in heaven.***" Matthew 16:19. We are in control but few realize it!

How do we stay on track? Our Manual tells us, "***And be not conformed to this world: but be ye transformed by the renewing of your mind, that ye may prove what is that good, and acceptable, and perfect, will of God.***" Romans 12:2. We actually control the spirit realm every day by the words we choose to speak and spiritual laws we violate. "***But grow in grace, and in the knowledge of our Lord and Savior Jesus Christ...***" II Peter 3:18. As we constantly increase in knowledge of His Word *–which is through meditation–* it will keep infections like the enemy at **bay**. Without the Word of God as a track to run on, our mind will be susceptible to his influence. "***A double minded man is unstable in all his ways.***" James 1:8.

The Misconception of Being Saved

This subheading above will probably initiate some very controversial thoughts and criticism especially by mature believers who feel they are knowledgeable in the faith. Why, because it will birth several questions:

> First, is there a misconception?
> Secondly, am I really saved?
> Finally, can I lose my salvation?

It is critical to point out, from God's standpoint, there is permanency of salvation provided which is available to everyone. However, whose responsibility is it to keep themselves in-line? The liability falls entirely on a believer. "...***keep yourself pure.***" I Timothy 5:22. God even went the extra mile and made provisions just in case we derail, slip-up or fall off course. We can even get back in-line with God by asking for forgiveness and acknowledging Him in all that we do; this is why the Scripture reveals to us, "***Trust in the LORD with all your heart, and lean not on your own understanding; in all your ways acknowledge Him, And He shall direct your paths.***" Proverbs 3:5-6.

However, there is a vital role all believers play whether they remain on-track with God or choose to **re**turn to worldly pleasures they once enjoyed. In conversation, you may or will hear the phrase '**once**

saved, always saved.' Or, "I cannot lose my salvation no matter what I do. This statement is usually supported by one of the most powerful Scripture verse in the entire Word of God. It is John 3:16. "***For God so loved the world that He gave His only begotten Son, that whoever believes in Him should not perish but have everlasting life.***" However, let us take a look at another premier verse which also mentioned by the same writer *–John–* surrounding **eternal** life. "***Whoever hates his brother is a murderer, and you know that no murderer has eternal life abiding in him.***" I John 3:15. What an eye opener!

First, we must ask ourselves, is this latter Scripture directed to the world or to the body of Christ? As you can clearly observe, both verses have 'everlasting or eternal' life in them. How about John's third and monumental statement surrounding what God says is man's choice and rights. "***I know your works, that you are neither cold nor hot. I could wish you were cold or hot. So then, because you are lukewarm, and neither cold nor hot, I will vomit you out of My mouth.***" Revelations 3:15-16.

The focal point comes down to a person's lifestyle. We cannot say we are saved: yet, we hate our brother or sister. This is like walking in the middle of the road in our relationship with God! As you know it is the most dangerous place to be! We cannot conduct ourselves as before and still go to be with The Lord. This would be like a criminal who still engages in criminal activities but thinks he is exempt from judicial consequence, punishment or imprisonment. Now do you see why the misconception of permanency needs to always be clarified and placed in its proper order?

All who venture through God's canal of salvation in Jesus and maintain a proper lifestyle will see God. "***Blessed are the pure in heart: for they shall see God.***" Matthew 5:8. If a believer sins, they are to ask the Lord for forgiveness ASAP and turn from the sin, in order to be placed back on the eternal path. God gave us a directive which says, " ***let not the sun go down upon your wrath***..." Ephesians 4:26. We are about to unveil another classical line some believers mention. They state, "**I am a work in progress.**" What, after twenty years of knowing, reading God's Word, laying on of hands to heal, and interacting with mature believers, they have still not gotten it right? Did we mention this 'work-in-progress' statement to their employer after (90) days? How about a spouse who got caught cheating? I guess if you were a business owner and had standards in place, you would tolerate someone's error no matter how long they take to get things right. Also, I wonder if God will tolerate us for constantly repeating the same transgression day-after-day and year after year. Beloved, we cannot choose to live by our own standard, hold prejudice, hate others, watch pornography, use illegal drugs/alcohol, hurt innocent children, sleep around, practice bestiality and think God understands. He is a Holy God and requires His offspring to live holy as well! God's plan of salvation is of a permanent nature; whether we continue to carry–out His standards to the end or not, is a whole different story. Again, Jesus said, "***Let your light so shine before men, that they may see your good works, and glorify your Father which is in heaven***." Matthew 5:16.

While we live on earth, there is diligent work to be done and many hurdles we have to scale before our soul will arrive at its ultimate destination. The Word of Life confirms, "***For we are made partakers of Christ, if we hold the beginning of our confidence steadfast unto the end***." Hebrews 3:14. What happens if we do not choose to hold on to the end? It is the same results if we do not hold onto the high standards in place and requirements of our jobs.

Let us conclude the misconception with the following; our soul will remain fixed on course towards eternity as long as we maintain a genuine love walk, forgive others and embrace a focused mind-set towards God in loving others. "***Since you have purified your souls in obeying the truth through the Spirit in sincere love of the brethren, love one another fervently with a pure heart.***" I Peter 1:22.

Awareness and Expectation

In the book of James, his letter was directed to the twelve churches of believers in Christ. He says, "***Therefore lay aside all filthiness and overflow of wickedness, and receive with meekness the implanted word, which is able to save your souls. But be doers of the word, and***

***not hearers only, deceiving yourselves.".*" James 1:21-22. Let us stop deceiving ourselves to think we can still reengage in debauchery and still go to Heaven to be with The Lord. Based on this line of reasoning, I guess Lucifer/satan, Cain, Judas, Ananias & Sapphira in Acts chapter five, Hymaneus and Alexander in I Timothy 1:20 are all properly aligned in God. The reasons why God directed James to say, '**lay aside**' –or avoid– is due to obstacles which can prevent believers from reaching maturity now and reaching their Godly destination later.

God made provisions of restoration just in case we stumbled or **un**-intentionally fell off course. You only avoid something if it will cause pain, hurt, hinder or obstruct progress, isn't that true? Again, it is only by faith anyone can say, 'I am saved', with the understanding that there are daily guidelines to continually live by, follow and uphold in order to obtain eternal life. This is the same requirement in our occupation we adhere to and follow their guidelines in order to maintain employment.

Being saved is not only a one-time belief and confession. We have to forgive others and conduct ourselves daily with a lifestyle well pleasing to Our Father. In doing so, we keep our soul on the right track. The Apostle Paul said, "*…**in Him we liv, move and have our being***." Acts 17:28. This new walk with Christ should be a daily high-profile life of forgiveness which are one of the top keys of the kingdom of God here on earth. God's Holy Spirit is here to assist us in both spiritual battles in the unseen realm and personal difficulties we face every day. Remember, "***Many are the afflictions of the righteous: but the LORD delivers him out of them all***." Psalms 34:19.

The Scripture directs us to, "***Trust in the LORD with all your heart, and lean not on your own understanding; in all your ways acknowledge Him, And He shall direct your paths***." Proverbs 3:5-6. As you know, there is work to be done in order to maintain the 'saved' status. God will never make choices for us but only provisions for His offspring just as a parent does for their children. If He did, then He becomes responsible for any adverse results.

The Word of Truth says, there are spiritual battles being fought both locally as well as over every country on earth. In the book of Daniel, it mentions that when the angel finally came to him, "***Then he said, "Do you know why I have come to you? And now I must return to fight with the prince of Persia; and when I have gone forth, indeed the prince of Greece will come.***" Daniel 10:20. The battles being fought in the spirit realm is for the most important part of our being which is the soul. Most children of God are not aware there is a real warfare taking place right in their midst which they think are natural occurrences. We are all in a serious spiritual war zone while we live here on earth. We are not living in a park playground of fun but a real spiritual atmosphere every day for the souls of men. As we know, the Scriptures often-times convey messages in military terms as it is mentioned in 2 Corinthians 11:26 and elsewhere.

- ***We wrestle <u>not against flesh and blood</u>.*** Ephesians 6:11.
- ***<u>Fight</u> a good fight*** II Timothy 4:7.
- ***We are <u>more than</u> conquerors.*** Romans 8:37.
- ***For the weapons of our warfare are <u>not carnal</u>*** ...II Cor. 10:4.
- ***He who overcomes***... Revelations 21:7.
- ***Therefore, take unto you <u>the whole armor</u> of God*** ... Eph. 6:13.

Listed above are detailed descriptions of what actually takes place every day while we live on earth interacting with others. There are situations we will frequently face and obstacles we <u>must</u> continually overcome. Obstacles and difficulties we face are not there to test the commitment of our faith but to reveal just what overcomers we are. They do reveal to us just how awesome we are as stewards who are identified with God. "***For our light affliction, which is but for a moment, is working for us a far more exceeding and eternal weight of glory;***" II Corinthians 4:17.

Notice, what we face is temporary but once it is overcome, it will work out something far better. Therefore, any challenge we face; God knows we can be the victor if we stay on track! Hence the reason for living a Godly lifestyle is so critical; it can attract others as well as bring God glory. We are His offspring and we are to live holy because He is Holy! "***But as He who called you is holy; you also be holy in <u>all</u> your conduct.***" I Peter 1:15. We do not want to be off course when

Christ appears to catch away His Saints. "***In a moment, in the twinkling of an eye, at the last trumpet. For the trumpet will sound, and the dead will be raised incorruptible, and we shall be changed***. I Corinthians 15:52. We are to equip (*arm*) ourselves daily with God's two-edged sword, so we can cut off worldly pleasures and appeals of this life so that they do not deceive us. The Scripture says, "***For though we walk in the flesh, we do not war according to the flesh***:" II Cor. 10:3. Again, our soul is the enemy's primary target to try and influence, not our body. The enemy knows once the mind changes course, the body will naturally follow-suit.

The Word of God speaks of; "...***among whom also we all once conducted ourselves in the lusts of our flesh, fulfilling the desires of the flesh and of the mind, and were by nature children of wrath, just as the others."*** Ephesians 2:3. What happens when we choose to fulfill our own desires first instead of applying God's standard? The result will force a change of direction away from Our Source. In order to prepare for the challenges ahead, we need to put God's Word into practice at every encounter. On this road of life, if we do not apply what we know, we can be easily enticed to take the quick exit towards revisiting passions and pleasures.

What Happens If Someone Dies Seconds After Receiving Christ?

The minute someone believes/confess Jesus as Lord (owner) of their life is the instant that *–if they died–* their soul will immediately be with the Lord. This is referring to their full consciousness which is their soul. " ...***we are confident, I say, and willing rather to be absent from the body, and to be present with the Lord***." II Corinthians 5:8. Also, when someone dies, their spirit, soul and body separates. If they lived for God, their soul *–the real conscious person–* will immediately go to be with the Lord. Their spirit will return to God as well but their body will be buried in the ground. ***See Luke 20:35-36***.

Keep in mind, **only** while we are alive in the body can a personal choice of salvation be made. "***And as it is appointed unto men once to die, but after this the judgment***:" Hebrews 9:27. Therefore, if we yield to temptation and various lust, we sever ties with our Heavenly

Father. And, while separated if our body dies, our soul will **not** arrive at its intended port which is Heaven. On the other hand, when an unbeliever dies there is, "***But a certain fearful looking for of judgment and fiery indignation***." Hebrews 10:27. As offspring, God does not want any of His children to die in sin but to live for Him. This is why the Scripture instructs children of light what to do if/when we sin. "***If we confess our sins, He is faithful and just to forgive us our sins and to cleanse us from all unrighteousness***." I John 1:9.

Notice, sin will cause us to become unrighteous. And, it is by confessing exactly what the sin is *–we have committed–* and turning from it which causes us to be cleansed from unrighteousness and placed back on proper alignment with God. However, in order for God to forgive us of our trespasses *–so we can be restored to the status of right standing–* it is imperative that any malice, jealousy, envy, hatred, or adverse thoughts against a brother or sister, it **must** be confessed to the Lord and/or the person ASAP.

Once this process is carried out, we are reinstated to Our Father God. "***For if you forgive men their trespasses, your heavenly Father will also forgive you. But if you do not forgive men their trespasses, neither will your Father forgive your trespasses.***" Matthew 6:14-15. The Scripture clearly tells ambassadors for Christ: "***since you have purified your souls in obeying the truth through the Spirit in sincere love of the brethren, love one another fervently with a pure heart***." I Peter 1:22. In other words, our soul can become defiled and contaminated. God does not want us to carry the baggage of un-forgiveness, malice and hatred on board our destination towards eternal life.

Whose responsibility is it to purify the soul? Ours! How do we cleanse our souls? It is done by obeying the truth through the spirit by demonstrating *–not just love but–* sincere love for each other without hypocrisy. What if we do not love? Simple, God does not live in us. "***He who does not love does not know God, for God is love.***" 1 John 4:8.

Do not be deceived, there are always directives *–even on our earthly jobs–* which are our responsibility to constantly uphold. This is so regardless of when the death of our body occurs, our soul will immediately be with the Lord. Again, "***we are confident, yes, well pleased rather to be absent from the body and to be present with the Lord***. II Corinthians 5:8.

Our Soul Comprises of our Mind, Desires and Emotions

As we continue to first forgive others and demonstrate fervent love towards them, we will remain in right standing with God. You have probably heard teachings of what the soul is and its functions. When or, if doubt surfaces, we are to ask our Father to reveal the truth to us by the Holy Spirit. Some have been taught or have heard of the soul as being the unconscious mind as mentioned previously. And, others teach that the soul encompasses the mind, **will** and emotions.

Let us start by saying, regardless of what we may have been taught, heard or thought of the soul and its function, the Scripture discloses it is the very essence of our being. "***And do not fear those who kill the body but cannot kill the soul,"*** Matthew 10:28. Also, Jesus said***, "For what profit is it to a man if he gains the whole world, and loses his own soul? Or what will a man give in exchange for his soul?"*** Matthew 16:26. Please take a closer look at the high value Jesus places on man's soul.

After our soul has been introduced to God's Word, it even plays a more significant role in our relationship with God than our spirit. By the way, the spirit of every human who has ever lived whether good or evil, their spirit will always return to God who gave it. "***Then the dust will return to the earth as it was, And the spirit will return to God who gave it***." Ecclesiastes 12:7. However, the real you *-as it relates to eternity-* is not your spirit but your soul. Not every question you have may be answered with the information we provide about the soul.

However, beginning at this stage in your life, the knowledge you acquire about your composition is designed to establish a more secure foundation on which you can start living a fulfilled life. God wants you to acquire more knowledge about yourself and your potential. Again, our soul comprises our **mind**, **desires** and **emotions**, which can all be expressed and exercised through our physical body. We will detail each aspect briefly with scriptural reference to help further your understanding of the soul.

Concerning Our Mind

The Word of Truth says, "***For who has known the mind of the LORD that he may instruct Him? but we have the mind of Christ*** " 1 Corinthians 2:16. And, "***for God has not given us a spirit of fear, but of power and of love and of a sound mind***." II Timothy 1:7. Also, "***For to be carnally minded is death, but to be spiritually minded is life and peace***." Romans 8:6.

Next, "…***And do not be conformed to this world, but be transformed by the renewing of your mind, that you may prove what is that good and acceptable and perfect will of God***." Romans 12:2. Finally, "a***nd be renewed in the spirit of your mind***." Ephesians 4:23. Notice the strong emphasis all these verses place on our mind. We can see it is of extreme importance and precise detail which it expresses. However, if our mind is not constantly *–daily–* being replenished by its fuel *–The Word of God–* our perception of Him and of sin will become clouded. The result will be our pathways can become foggy so we cannot see or perceive any snares set for us by the adversary.

The constant renewing is like the scheduled maintenance cars require. For example, if we allow our cars to constantly run near empty before refueling, sediments and dirt can easily clog the filters or injectors which can cause poor performance. As children of the Most-High, we are advised to filter out substances which the Word of God says to discard like envy, pornography, illicit sex, hatred, illegal drug, alcohol and malice. This is so that when we are called to run a race set before us, we will not be like the five foolish virgins who did not fill up their lamps when they had the opportunity.

The result was that they were left behind. ***See Matthew 25: 1-13***. God's Word constrains us to have a "***ready mind***." II Cor. 8:19. This also means to be on-call like doctors or, to always be ready to minister God's saving grace at a moment's notice. It is important to note that our eyes provide the portal and appeal to our mind; they become partners and can either work together or break our fellowship with The Lord. Remember 'the lust of the eyes' can cause our mind to runaground like ships, be enticed or lead us to fulfill ungodly desires. Remember, "***The eye is not satisfied with seeing***" Ecclesiastes. 1:8. We are to discard appeals if they hinder our relationship with God's Holy Spirit. This way, we will be able to see clearly and not have to question whether we have to stop for refueling, filter change or tire pressure check.

Concerning Our Desires

In order for us to comprehend the full nature of 'desire,' let us go back to the beginning in The Garden of Eden so we can properly study its origin. Then, we will be able to distinguish what personal versus Godly desires are and the role each plays in our lives collectively. The Word of Life tells us after Eve **saw** "…***and a tree desirable to make one wise***" -*Genesis 3:6*- she ate and gave to her husband. Eve's desire eventually led them both to transgress against God. Now this does not mean 'desires' are evil, it simply means desires are powerful and therefore, need restraint. God's Manual about life says, "***among whom also we all once conducted ourselves in the lusts of our flesh, fulfilling the desires of the flesh and of the mind, and were by nature children of wrath, just as the others***." Ephesians 2:3.

The Scripture goes on to mention, once we have entered a relationship with God *–through Jesus the Christ–* our desires should be directed toward winning our neighbors and co-workers, friends and people to Him. This is why Jesus called us, "fishers of men." Mark. 1:17. In our calling, we are fulfilling the work He has for us to accomplish here on earth. Remember in chapter one it said, "***as newborn babes, desire the pure milk of the word, that you may grow thereby***." 1 Peter 2:2. Then it says, "***Pursue love, and desire spiritual gifts***." 1 Corinthians 14:1. After that, it tells us, "***Therefore, I say unto you what things soever you desire*** …" Mark 11:24.

Also, "***Delight yourself also in the LORD, and He shall give you the desires of your heart***." Psalms 37:4. Some believers do not realize that their desire precedes action. Now let us read James' detailed contribution on this subject matter. "***Then, when desire has conceived, it gives birth to sin; and sin, when it is full-grown, brings***

forth death." James 1:15. Please note the sequence from desire to demise/death. So then, before 'desire' can make its debut, a degree of understanding has to be acquired. When the Scripture says, '*desire*', it is directed to the soul of man. To desire is to crave or long for something. It is good to note that both our soul and our flesh have desires. The difference is the desire of the flesh is to obtain what is personally gratifying for immediate sensual or physical satisfaction whereas, the renewed mind craves for the nourishment needed to continually strengthen the rest of the composition for the long haul. This is so it can effectively carry out the directives from God. Whenever I minister in a group setting, I usually start out by asking the following question. "What is the one thing you must do every day?" The answers usually vary; then I bring them back to the Word of God; I mention the answer is found in Joshua 24:15 which is '**choice**' or, "***choose this day whom you will serve.***"

The things we desire will usually lead us to make a choice. Did you know, at the last supper when Jesus sat with His twelve disciples, He said "...***with desire I have desired to eat this Passover with you before I suffer***..." Luke 22:15. Jesus, who is God's perfect revelation of Himself in the flesh -*Colossians 1:15*- chose to spend the last hours of mortality with His disciples. Again, our desires will always lead us to make choices in the works God has for us to do on earth.

We are to steer –*direct*– our desires toward participating in eternal things, so our personal and temporary desires become less-and-less appealing. This is why John the Baptist said, "...***He must increase but I must decrease***." John 3:30. Not only was John talking about Jesus' ministry, but also of his own desire to see more of the works of God manifested in his cousin Jesus. A person's desire to put into practice the things of God comes from the information –*word*– he or she **chooses** to read, believe and act upon.

Concerning the Emotions

The emotions of man is a rarely mentioned area of ministry. We will use one person to pinpoint two separate situations. The Apostle Peter demonstrated both positive and negative aspects. Peter's first emotional outburst was before he was empowered by God's Holy

Spirit. Do you recall his response to the prophecy Jesus gave of His upcoming sacrificial death? "***And He began to teach them that the Son of Man must suffer many things, and be rejected by the elders and chief priests and scribes, and be killed, and after three days rise again. He spoke this word openly. Then Peter took Him aside and began to rebuke Him. But when He had turned around and looked at His disciples, He rebuked Peter, saying, "Get behind Me, Satan! For you are not mindful of the things of God, but the things of men."*** Mark 8:31-33. Peter displayed the concern of a leader who saw Jesus' death as something inappropriate for the present time because of the miraculous and overwhelming effect of His ministry. This display of pure human emotions and feelings of compassion was without a comprehensive understanding of God's ultimate plan of man's redemption.

Peter's reprimand of Jesus' forecast was met with rebuke and disciplinary action. We know this situation required spiritual perception not an emotional outburst. The new description of the emotion comes into being when someone is empowered by the Holy Spirit and continues to increase in the knowledge of God. Peter fits this description as well. The Scripture says, "***Now when they saw the boldness of Peter and John, and perceived that they were uneducated and untrained men, they marveled. And they realized that they had been with Jesus***." Acts 4:13. Emotions which are directed or used in service and/or worship towards God is called **zeal**.

Zeal is a diligent devotion, eagerness or passion, which embraces an impersonal concern. It is also a consciousness which is able to discern and exercise God's plan regardless of the present condition. The Scripture says, *–Jesus–* "***who gave Himself for us, that He might redeem us from every lawless deed and purify for Himself His own special people, zealous for good works***." Titus 2:14. Some believers think it is wrong to be emotional, but remember, God made us with emotions. As you've read above, Peter came to find out that emotional responses *–in spiritual matters–* are wrong only if they obstruct or hinder God's ultimate plan.

Next there was Saul of Tarsus whose name Jesus changed to Paul after his conversion. He acted with zeal to imprison or kill those who called on Jesus and the 'new way.' As you know, he persecuted believers in Christ. "***And I punished them oft in every synagogue, and compelled them to blaspheme; and being exceedingly mad against them, I persecuted them even unto strange cities***. Acts 26:11. When worshipping God, there can be both zeal and emotions which God honors because it brings Him glory. This includes **joy** in the things of the Lord. ***See Isaiah 61:10, Luke 10:17***. **Boldness**. Acts 4:31. **Tears** John 11:35, II Timothy 1:3-4. This also includes **praises and even dancing** before the Lord as David did. ***See Psalms 150:4 and II Samuel 6:14***. Almost all emotions are finally expressed through our physical body whether personal or Godly. This is why the two can easily be confused if we do not use the Word of God to separate and detail them independently.

"***For the Word of God is alive and powerful, and sharper than any two-edged sword, piercing even to the division of soul and spirit, and of joints and marrow, and is a discerner of the thoughts and intents of the heart."*** Hebrews 4:12. Now let us go back to the 'good works' mentioned above in **Titus 2:14**. And, while we look forward to doing 'good works', there will always be emotions or zeal involved whether personal or Godly. Again, we are **not** to make decisions based on our personal emotions while involved in the works of God. We are to ask the Lord for revelation in our encounters and use the answer as our navigator or guide.

In Luke's account and Peter's summary of Jesus' ministry, he said, "***how God anointed Jesus of Nazareth with the Holy Spirit and with power; who went about doing good, and healing all that were oppressed of the devil; for God was with him***." Acts 10:38. The zeal towards good works was apparent throughout Jesus' ministry as well as with the apostles. We are never to confuse zeal with feelings. Our physical body allows us to feel and sense our environment personally but we are not to rely exclusively on what we feel but on what is revealed by His Holy Spirit.

God gave us emotions to work in conjunction with our regenerated spirit so we could wholly serve Him with all our being. The Scripture says, "***And you shall love the LORD your God with all your heart, with all your soul, with all your mind, and with all your strength.'***

This is the first commandment." Mark 12:30. And, as we mentioned earlier, personal feelings and concerns can change as easily as the wind changes direction which makes them very unstable. Most mature believers do not allow their feelings or sympathy to lead them to make spiritual decisions even for themselves.

Is Our Will Part of Our Soul?

This subtitle is a common question most people have about the soul. Yet, some are either afraid to address it or they repeat what others have taught them. Please do not be confused to think your soul is your 'will.' Your 'will' is a state or plateau to which you can arrive. Your 'will', has to come into play through information filtered from the soul.

This means your 'will' is NOT a stand-alone entity; neither does it exist independently. Our desires can bring into existence the "will." However, our "will" cannot bring into existence desires. There is no 'will' without desire. Our 'will' can make up an intricate part of our soul. Another important facet of the soul is that there are four avenues which must be present before we arrive at your 'will. They are as follows:

1. ***Information*** and understanding have to be acquired and/or revealed about a subject. Then,
2. A calculated ***choice*** has to be made based on personal understanding, influence, past experience and/or revelation.
3. Then, a ***desire*** comes into play to carry out what was chosen.
4. Finally, a ***determination*** can then be made because of our foreknowledge, information and/or beliefs.

After our soul has sifted through all the four (4) pertinent functions – *in a fraction of a second or over a period of time*– this is when we arrive at the "**will.**" Our will is like our physical heart which has arteries and veins leading both to and from. Therefore, our heart, in our chest cavity, is not a lone entity because it does not function without support. By the same token, our will has (4) 'arteries' which are: information, choice, desire and determination leading to it as well.

Our determination becomes the major artery into the arena of the '**will**'. Let us see how Jesus clearly demonstrated these characteristics surrounding the **will.** Remember, He came with information to carry out His Father's **plan**; He said, "***for I have come down from heaven not to do mine own will but the will of Him that sent me***." John 6:38. Going forward, when we think of "**will**," it is best if we associate it with the word '**purpose**.'

In order for us to carry out someone else's plan, the four mentioned criteria must be met. As a result, given the necessary data, our 'will' can lead our spirit to work in harmony even if it means to sacrifice the body unto death. Again, Jesus should always be both our primary and default example. God knew in order for mankind to be rescued from where they landed, a final sacrifice had to be made, innocent blood had to be shed, and Jesus' body had to die so His spirit and soul could properly carry out their detailed functions. "***Therefore He says: "When He ascended on high, He led captivity captive, And gave gifts to men***." Ephesians 4:8.

Jesus clearly understood His purpose on earth because He had the **information** *–plan–* which was constructed jointly with His Father to redeem man back to Himself. Jesus made the **choice** to sacrifice His physical life. And, by doing so, He was able to effectively carry out His Father's plan by His own **desire**.

Finally, Jesus made the **determination** to remain unmovable even when He was beaten, spat- upon, beard pulled-out and knew he was facing certain death. By Jesus' victory over what man did to God's order/laws, He would fulfill an even greater purpose of carrying out His Father's plan of redemption for generations to come. Beloved, Jesus has now provided the avenue to legally redeem all of mankind back to His Father if they choose to believe and confess Him as Lord.

Jesus provided the access; He said, "***I am the way, the truth, and the life. No one comes to the Father except through Me***." John 14:6.

Individual Review or Class Discussion

1—The word **SAVED** mean to____________ or to_____________

S.A.V.E as an acronym is:

2—Which part of our composition does **SAVE** apply?

3—Please explain/write-out what it means to be **saved**?

4—Please explain why it would not be fair to all if a person can obtain salvation by their own efforts?

5—When someone is saved, does it mean they **cannot** lose their salvation? **T/F.** Please state your view as well as God's view.

1.

2.

6—Is the following statement true; our soul is made up of our mind, will and emotions? **T/F**; if false, explain:

7—Can someone claim to know God but God does **not** know them?

Please state either point.

Please explain:

Turn to: Matt. 7:22-23.

Chapter IV-----------→ *Converted*

This section on conversion is **<u>not</u>** widely taught yet, it is vitally important to understand throughout the intricate process of salvation. As we know, the word converted means to be changed, adopted or made suitable for something new. We know it was man's relationship with God which was altered as a result of Adam's transgression approximately six thousand years ago and the lingering effects are still born in all human genetics today.

Evidence of which states, "***For since by man came death, by Man also came the resurrection of the dead. For as in Adam all die, even so in Christ all shall be made alive.***" I Corinthians 15:21-22. This means we can become alive again so that we can reconnect to God spiritually the way Adam was prior to his fall.

Let us provide a detailed and profound description using an acronym to point-out what converted encompasses; converted means to:

C-hange
O-ld
N-egative
V-iew *of*
E-xistence *and*
R-each
T-owards
E-ternal
D-estiny

As it is spelled out, conversion involves a real change of mind-set with a new view of eternity as the destination. Before we move forward, we would like to ask a question which yields the seemingly obvious answer. It is, where did God place man after he was created? The apparent answer is the Garden of Eden. The more conscious answer is '**<u>in His presence</u>**.' Some believers may not be aware that man was actually placed in a garden eastward in Eden. **See Genesis 2:8**. God desires us to be reconnected *–reborn–* for better spiritual experience. In order to be effective, we are to change the old negative view and envision ourselves as eventually ruling and reigning with Christ.

"And hath made us <u>kings</u> and <u>priests</u> unto God and his Father; to him be glory and dominion forever and ever. Amen" Revelations 1:6. This is all part of our new outlook and why proper understanding of God's Word is so critical. As we know, Jesus' physical presence was to personally demonstrate the power of conversion so that we would observe a physical example *–Himself–* to be our ultimate model.

Why would a Holy God require anything less of His ultimate creation which is man? God, who is Holy, desires man to get '**the right memo**' ASAP and become familiar once again with their Source. During my time of ministering to others, whether individually or teaching a Bible Study class, I have been met with ridicule and rejection when I mention, 'it is about a new mindset because we don't have to sin, we choose to sin!'

Think back on our job(s); how many times did our boss or manager give us a directive and we chose to do something contrary? Wouldn't it seem futile if after we confess Jesus as Lord, we constantly reverted to our past and there was no evidence of change? You see beloved, when someone agrees that Jesus is Lord of their life, there is a status change and new instructions provided just like your previous Job provided guidelines. We are all fully aware when we transgress or yield to sin; sin never surprises us or comes up behind us and hits us over the head!

This is why the Word of Truth challenges and reveals to us our new capabilities. "***For sin shall not have dominion over you***." Romans 6:14. Did you know Jesus told someone, "…***go, and sin no more***?" John 8:11. This verse provides both the example and new outlook to grasp because of a new plateau of information. "***But now being made free from sin, and become servants to God, you have your fruit unto holiness, and the end everlasting life***." Romans 6:22. We are to choose to live above the pleasures of sin realizing that we have been given new capabilities, directives and expectations. From this day forward, let us exercise control over sin and show it who's boss! Sin does not rule us anymore; we are now in full control. As most of us are aware, God's Word has an answer to every problem/condition.

The Inclusion of All (4) Terms; repent, born-again, saved and <u>converted</u>

As a believer, the most important aspect throughout the entire salvation experience is understanding how our composition *–spirit, soul and body–* **fits** together seamlessly. It is critical that we as offspring grasp all that salvation encompasses so that we are confident in knowing who we are in Christ in God. First, we are to know how conversion relates to our eternal **spirit**. Then, the way it affects our personal **soul**; finally, how it applies to our physical **body** collectively.

It is vital we become more aware of conversion. The reason is that it details we are really **spirit** beings who possess a **soul** and live in a physical **body**. "***Now may the God of peace Himself sanctify you completely; and may your whole spirit, soul, and body be preserved blameless at the coming of our Lord Jesus Christ***." I Thessalonians 5:23. This is significant because the conversion process touches all **three** aspects of our being; seen below.

• Spirit

Our **spirit** is the part of us which God breathed *–birth–* out of Himself. ***-See Genesis 2:7-***. Then, He blew His breath into man's nostril *-nose-* and man became a living soul.

• Soul

Our **soul** consists of the mind, the desires and the emotions which we develop throughout this life. And, it is our personal and true unique identity as a human being. Everyone's soul is as unique as a fingerprint. Our soul is our most valuable asset according to Jesus in Matthew 6:26, Mark 8:36. The soul is housed in our physical body.

• Body

The **Body** is the physical entity God made out of the dirt or ground mixed with water. ***See Genesis 2:7***. This clay-statue or configuration was ultimately constructed to house God's Holy Spirit along with our genetics and eternal spirit from God. By the way, the name Adam means red earth, dark earth or ruddy, **not** 'first man.'

God calls our body a temple because it has now become the only legal dwelling agency for Himself here on earth. "***Or do you not know that your body is the temple of the Holy Spirit who is in you, whom you have from God, and you are not your own?"*** 1 Corinthians. 6:19. As some of us are aware, God does not and has not dwelled in temples – *buildings*– made by hands since Jesus' appearance over two thousand years ago. God only comes into a building if you, the believer, is there! Further evidence confirms. "***However, the Most High does not dwell in temples made with hands, as the prophet says***." Acts 7:48.

With our body not belonging to us any longer, the Word of God says we are to yield to the ultimate teacher and guide who is His Holy Spirit. "***For as many as are led by the Spirit of God, they are the sons of God***." Romans 8:14. We are to become more familiar with what Jesus said about His Holy Spirit. "***But the Comforter, which is the Holy Spirit, whom the Father will send in my name, He shall teach you all things, and bring all things to your remembrance, whatsoever I have said unto you***." John 14:26.

Conversion Is the Restoration of our minds to its Original State

First things first! "***For who hath known the mind of the Lord, that he may instruct him? But we have the mind of Christ***." I Corinthians 2:16. Jesus said, "***Verily I say unto you, except you be converted, and become as little children, you shall not enter into the kingdom of heaven***." Matthew 18:3. When we digest the Word of Truth as the source to transform our thinking, we place ourselves on the track of His righteousness.

21"And you, who once were alienated and enemies in your mind by wicked works, yet now He has reconciled

22 in the body of His flesh through death, to present you holy, and blameless, and above reproach in His sight.

23 if indeed you continue in the faith, grounded and steadfast, and

are not moved away from the hope of the gospel which you heard, which was preached to every creature under heaven, of which I, Paul, became a minister. Colossians 1:21-23. Before sin got ahold of man, there was perfect unity, holiness, innocence, sharpness of mind and union with the Father. The Scripture says, "***Repent therefore and be converted, that your sins may be blotted out, so that times of refreshing may come from the presence of the Lord.***" Acts 3:19. There are some widespread rumors and teachings that someone does not have to change or be properly aligned with God in order to have a right relationship with Him.

This is the height of deception and a perversion of truth, which is like a mirage. No one can engage in unrighteousness and still be righteous before a Holy God; **this may be someone's personal theory but not according to Scripture!** And, it is why the Scriptures require a daily decision by every believer to; "***Choose you this day who you will serve.***" Joshua 24:15.

As enlightened stewards, we are to choose to turn away from sin when it approaches which is when a refreshing time can take its place. "***For the hearts of this people have grown dull. Their ears are hard of hearing, And their eyes they have closed, Lest they should see with their eyes and hear with their ears, Lest they should understand with their hearts and turn, So that I should heal them.***" Matthew 13:15.

God desires all His children to have a good life experience so that they can look forward to bearing fruit for others to enjoy. We have written the following verse numerous times throughout this book because it is so critical to our development. "***And do not be conformed to this world, but be transformed by the renewing of your mind, that you may prove what is that good and acceptable and perfect will of God.***" Romans 12:2.

Conversion describes the change which takes place in our spirit and our minds. "...***that, in reference to your former manner of life, you lay aside the old self, which is being corrupted in accordance with the lusts of deceit.***" Ephesians 4:22. In other words, whatever conclusion someone comes to on his or her own will never precede God's standard. God simply requires obedience and adherence to His Word. In doing so, we can be a light unto others who are in darkness.

Always remember, if we do not change the way we think, we will never change the way we are. The Scripture confirms this by stating, "***For as he thinks in his heart, so is he.***" Proverbs 23:7. After being changed, God sees us as holy, righteous without blame and not being held liable for our past rejection of His Word. Now that we have been **re**introduced to God and given the roadmap GPS back to Him, the Scripture says we are to, "***...walk in a manner worthy of the God who calls you into His own kingdom and glory...***" I Thessalonians 2:12. This means to stay on track!

God Introduced Conversion as A Result of Adam's High Treason

After God created Adam and Eve and placed them in a Garden eastward in Eden, He told them what tree they should not eat from; "***for in the day that you eat of it you shall surely die.***" Genesis 2:17. However, after they disobeyed God and ate of the tree of knowledge of good and evil, Adam went on living physically for over nine hundred and thirty years. Did God lie concerning 'the day'? Of course not! God **cannot** lie. "...***in hope of eternal life which God, who cannot lie, promised before time began.***" Titus 1:2. God who is Spirit, sees man's death as being spiritually disconnected from Him –*The Source* and Sustainer– which we all perceive as a physical demise.

The crime they committed was called treason. Treason is the act of betrayal of one's country. You see, Adam actually owned earth and all its splendor. Adam did not realize what he had because he did not know who he was. The same is true for most people today because if someone does not know who they are, why they were created, or their family's spiritual lineage, they will naturally default into sin. Our enemy's job is to try and keep humans ignorant of who they really are in God. Did you know the first test of man by the enemy was a knowledge check of what they knew and remembered?

The enemy asked Eve, "***has God said***...?" Genesis 3:1. As you know, they failed miserably and legally deeded over all that God gave them. As humans, things have not changed; we still have an identity crisis problem just like Adam and Eve. If Adam knew who he was, when the enemy tempted him, he should have stated, '***I am already like God***!' See Genesis 3:5. After they chose to yield to sin, the eternal part of them *–their spirit–* was immediately separated from God. Sin interfered with the part of them which is designed to share a deep communion with the Godhead. Therefore, it caused an eviction from the garden. "***So He drove out the man; and he placed at the east of the garden of Eden Cherubims, and a flaming sword which turned every way, to keep the way of the tree of life***." Genesis 3:24. This is why their soul and body had to accompany their spirit in departing from the presence of the Lord. Sin not only derails us from reaching our destination but severs ties with Our Source and Sustainer God.

Today, some denominations teach that after the death of the body, there exists only a state of stupor or sleep without consciousness. This is not true according to God's Word. Jesus contradicts this lie and theory when He said, "***For in the resurrection they neither marry nor are given in marriage, but are like angels of God in heaven.***" Matthew 22:30. This means only one aspect is placed back in the ground; the other parts/entities of our composition still lives-on forever! By the way, a **marriage** *–as underlined above–* and divorce can both be properly defined and appropriated as follows: it is a, /to:

M-utual	**D**-ivide &
A-rrangement	**I**-ntentionally
R-equiring	**V**-iolate *an*
R-ighteousness &	**O**-ath *by*
I-ntimacy	**R**-enouncing
A-fter	**C**-hrist's
G-od's	**E**-xample
E-xample	

The primary subjects in the verse above are resurrection and **marriage**. This is the highest order of a relationship on earth because it was initiated and designed by God between a heterosexual male and a female. Jesus even related marriage to saints/church today as a spiritual union called the bride of Christ. The union between a man and a woman is the ultimate transformation because they convert to one flesh. The Word of God specifically says, "***husbands, love your***

***wives, even as Christ also loved the church, and gave himself for it*." Ephesians 5:25. Very few understand the magnitude of marriage as it relates to the conversion process. Again, Jesus parallels marriage to His church which is His body. However, the way marriage is viewed today is totally against God's brilliant design. It has now been replaced with selfish ambitions, manipulation and lust supported by 'spirit of error.' The enemy's motive is to desecrate and insult what is God's highest **standard** among humans and His church.

As we stated earlier, the Scripture says, "***And GOD saw that the wickedness of man was great in the earth, and that every imagination of the thoughts of his heart was only evil continually*." Genesis 6:5. According to God's Word, these deviations are to emasculate man who God designed as the priest of the home, provider, the protector, instructor of children and prime example to the family for generations to come. An unholy definition of MARRIAGE is to:

M-ove
A-gainst
R-ighteousnes &
R-un
I-nto
A-buse of
G-od's
E-xample

When we do not understand the purpose or use of something or someone, we will abuse it/them. Beloved, going back to the conversion experience, it is about a new understanding and mindset once we confess Jesus as Lord. The Scripture confirms, "***that if you confess with your mouth the Lord Jesus and believe in your heart that God has raised Him from the dead, you will be saved. For with the heart one believes unto righteousness, and with the mouth confession is made unto salvation.***" Romans 10:9-10. Our personal confession of Jesus Christ and belief in God's Word creates the change in us which makes us more pliable to Him. Hence the reason we are called "His offspring." The sacrifice of God's only begotten son was the price paid for our personal choice to deviate from the standard. This is why He had to provide a means of reconciliation to Him! By the way, God honors the commitment Eunuchs make as well.

Conversion and the Holy Spirit

"***But the anointing which you have received from Him abides in you, and you do not need that anyone teach you; but as the same anointing teaches you concerning all things, and is true, and is not a lie, and just as it has taught you, you will abide in Him.*"** 1 John 2:27. We have mentioned this verse several times because it epitomizes the detailed works God's awesome Holy Spirit can do in every believer's life. ***"...after that you believed, you were sealed with that Holy Spirit of promise***." Ephesians 1:13.

Despite the clarity of the information presented, there will definitely be some situations which may arise in your life -*whether major or minor*- that you might never understand. And, some may even question the Lord as to why. However, God revealed the following: "***And we know that all things work together for good to those who love God, to those who are the called according to His purpose***." Romans 8:28. From now on, we are **not** to allow anything that happens in our life or in someone else's, to change our direction from reading and desiring to know more about the ultimate teacher, His Holy Spirit.

The apostle Paul said, "***for I am persuaded that neither death nor life, nor angels nor principalities nor powers, nor things present nor things to come, nor height nor depth, nor any other created thing, shall be able to separate us from the love of God which is in Christ Jesus our Lord***." Romans 8:38-39. Basically, all kinds of unforeseen things will happen; and, we may never know why. However, we are to keep the focus and not be distracted. The good news is, the things which occur in a believer's life are not by coincidence or luck. Neither are the bad things in a non-believer's life by destiny.

Once we choose to employ conversion, God's Holy Spirit is available. This is why Jesus said, "***But the Helper, the Holy Spirit, whom the Father will send in My name, He will teach you all things, and bring to your remembrance all things that I said to you.***" John 14:26. As we engage Him into our circumstance, He will instruct us. Remember the acronym "GREAT" mentioned back in chapter two about the specific works of the Holy Spirit in our daily lives? Again, He will:

G uide you into **all** truth.......................................John 16:13
R emind you of **all** things.......................................John 14:26
E mpower you to act on earth on Heaven's behalf..............Acts 1:8
A bide in you because you are God's temple on earth......I Cor. 6:18
T each you **all** things as a believer in Christ................John 14:26

On the other hand, to those in the world without Christ, His work is still prevalent on earth. "***and when He has come, He will convict the world of sin, and of righteousness, and of judgment.***" John 16:8. Today, God's gifts and administrations are distributed only as His Holy Spirit sees fit. "***But one and the same Spirit works all these things, distributing to each one individually as He wills.***" I Corinthians 12:11. God designed us to be lights in the world so that we expose darkness and exemplify holiness wherever we go. The Holy Spirit is the person of God who is available to build us up and teach us if we ask Him.

Conversion and Communion

When we think of communion *–which symbolically represents the breaking of the body and the shedding of the blood of Christ–* in the relationship to believers, Jesus gives us a detailed outline at His last supper with His disciples. The Scripture reminds us, "***and when He had given thanks, He broke it and said, "Take, eat; this is My body which is broken for you; do this in remembrance of Me. In the same manner He also took the cup after supper, saying, "This cup is the New Covenant in My blood. This do, as often as you drink it, in remembrance of Me.***" I Corinthians 11:24-26.

Jesus told His disciples by participating in this sacrament; you are demonstrating that you understand this portion of the New Covenant's arrangement. It is through the breaking of bread and the drinking from the cup which shows we remember His suffering. Later on in Scripture we see if communion is done ignorantly, its effect can cause premature death. We can read more about communion in its entirety. ***See I Corinthians 11:23-30.***

The apostle Paul shed further light on this subject matter when he attributed some –***physical and mental***– sickness, infirmities and even death to some who participated in communion ignorantly. The reason is, they did not understand its purpose. He said, "***For this cause many are weak and sickly among you, and many sleep***." I Corinthians 11:31.

Therefore, **unconverted** believers should never partake in communion because it will literally shorten their lifespan. Even today, if believers participate while stained with iniquity; the effects will be detrimental to their physical health as well. There are some people living today with various illnesses which no prescription can remedy; neither can any doctor cure them; even sincere prayer cannot provide healing if communion is taken without proper alignment with Christ. As strange as it may sound to some, communion is a spiritual function which can contribute to physical debility for those who are not aware of its potent effects. The same holds true of electricity; it can provide a multitude of needed functions but it can also kill you.

As stated above, we have to abide by God's conversion laws the same way we do electricity. Finally, parents –*who are exposed to this truth*– should prevent their young child(ren) from taking communion just to participate for ceremonial reasons. Just as we would not have a child to drink alcohol, take illegal drugs or do something which is potentially harmful or dangerous; neither should they be allowed to participate without correct spiritual understanding. The proper approach is to first lead them to Christ then, explain to them the reason for taking communion. This is the right approach parents and leaders are to take to ensure we are applying God's standard.

Summarizing the Whole Scope of Salvation

Now that we have separated, explained and detailed by chapters all that salvation entails, we will summarize the information to show how seamlessly God has designed them to fit together in our transformed life. First, let us touch briefly on the four key words which engulf God's perfect plan of salvation for mankind. We are going to provide in vivid and condensed summary how they all fit and apply to each part of man's composition which encompasses our spirit, soul and physical body on page 65. God desires everyone to be on the same plain of understanding. "***Till we all come in the unity of the faith, and of the knowledge of the Son of God, unto a perfect man, unto the measure of the stature of the fullness of Christ.***" Ephesians 4:13. God's love extends to all of mankind, bar none!

Repent

The specific order which surrounds salvation begins with one of the most important words and directive; it is **repent**. Remember, repent means to change the way we think and to reconsider what we have been exposed to in the past. Also, it means God originally designed mankind to go back to a high place in Him which means to be 'in His presence!' The meaning of repent parallels the word '**re**turn'; which we all know means to go back to the place we came from. Since mankind once occupied a high place with God, He desires all those in Christ to return there and experience life at the same plateau which Adam and Eve enjoyed before they transgressed.

Today, when someone repents *–by agreeing Jesus is Lord/Owner–* it creates a **mark** of identification on each believer's spirit by God's Holy Spirit. "***In Him you also trusted, after you heard the word of truth, the gospel of your salvation; in whom also, having believed, you were sealed with the Holy Spirit of promise.***" Ephesians 1:13. Repent is the first word both Jesus the Christ and John the Baptist mentioned at the inception of their ministries. And, it was intended to set in motion a transformation process which would turn their thought life and direction around.

Also, it would require that believers do **not** return to the pleasures of sin in the world but maintain a new course and disciplined lifestyle in Him. In other words, the new introduction to God would allow them to think differently in order to be placed on the right track of understanding, going forward. As far as the part of our composition where repent applies, it is to our minds not our body or spirit. The next significant area of our composition which the Word of God affects *–in a good way–* is our **spirit**. Everyone's spirit is dormant if they did NOT confess Jesus as Lord of their life.

Born Again

This is why Jesus said to Nicodemus you must be **born again** a second time spiritually in order to be able to enter and perceive the Kingdom of God mentally in his midst. When Jesus said, "***you must be born again***" in John 3:3-5, He was revealing that man's spirit was dormant *–since Adam's fall–* and it had to be rekindled or jump-started. Just as every human being has to be born through their earthly parents to come into this world to function physically, so must everyone experience this re-birth through their Heavenly Father's lineage to function effectively in His realm spiritually.

Our spirit is invisible to others, but it is a beacon of light to the real world of the spirit in which we are now authorized to function. And, it is the reason why Jesus said, "***you are the light of the world***." Matthew 5:14. Additional supporting evidence in Scripture says, "***having been born again, not of corruptible seed*** –parentage– ***but incorruptible, through the Word of God which lives and abides forever.***" 1 Peter 1:23. We were conceived the first time physically but have now been reborn spiritually through a nonphysical lineage so that our spirit could function the way God originally intended.

Our responsibility as converts is to maintain proper alignment with Our Father at all times because of a brand new understanding. This also means we have to be either hot or cold toward God's Word because He tolerates no middle ground. "***I know your works, that you are neither cold nor hot. I could wish you were cold or hot. So then, because you are lukewarm, and neither cold nor hot, I will vomit you out of My mouth***." Revelations 3:16. Let us ask a relevant question; where is the most dangerous part of any street or road? It is in the middle!

As friends of God, we actually choose where we stand in God at all times! The appearance of our spirit has the same outline as our physical body. The Apostle Paul stated, "***I know a man in Christ who fourteen years ago whether in the body I do not know, or whether out of the body I do not know, God know***…." 2 Corinthians 12:2. As children of the King, we are birthed with Our Father's characteristics so that we can live as highly elected officials called ambassadors for Christ, entrusted stewards and sons on the earth. "***Now we are ambassadors for Christ***..." II Corinthians 5:20. Again, the part of our composition where born again applies is only to our spirit not our body.

Saved

In this area following the re-birth of our spirit is the term/word **saved**. In order for us to be saved, there must be a savior. "***Neither is there salvation in any other, for there is no other name under heaven given among men by which we must be saved***." Acts 4:12. Beloved, our soul was derailed from the direction towards God. And, only God's Savior known as '**Christ Jesus the Lord**' can put us back on track. First, He will pick us up in our mess and introduce new information so that we can land in His spiritual arena. "...***and raised us up together, and made us sit together in the heavenly places in Christ Jesus***," Ephesians 2:6.

The term saved only refers to our soul. And God details how salvation comes about. Again, "***That if you confess with your mouth the Lord Jesus and believe in your heart that God has raised Him from the dead, you will be saved. For with the heart one believes unto righteousness, and with the mouth confession is made unto salvation***." Romans 10:9-10. The Word of God says our physical body *–is wonderfully made Psalms 139:14–* embodies both our soul and spirit. This makes us like the **Godhead** or three distinct entities which function in two realms with individually unique characteristics.

"***Now may the God of peace Himself sanctify you completely; and may your whole spirit, soul, and body be preserved blameless at the coming of our Lord Jesus Christ***."1 Thessalonians. 5:23. "***For there are three that bear witness in heaven: the Father, the Word, and the Holy Spirit; and these three are one***." 1 John 5:7. This is simply astounding; humans are now in a joint venture back with their Creator God. When we begin to grasp the magnitude of our make-up and the role each part of our composition plays in both realms, it literally goes beyond any natural comprehension.

Converted

The final arrival port encompasses what it means to be **changed**. In other words, conversion is a simple yet comprehensive understanding which wraps itself around the other three terms. As you know: they are repent, born again and saved. And, conversion envelops our spirit, soul and body's unique functions and characteristics. This allows them to be able to carry-out individual roles because they have all been exposed to God's Word. The Scripture confirms, "***Repent therefore and be converted, that your sins may be blotted out, so that times of refreshing may come from the presence of the Lord."*** Acts 3:19. When we look at the underlined words, it addresses a change, a renewal and an expected place.

As we pointed out earlier, our **soul** consists of our mind, desires and emotions which are our true identity as human beings. Also, God's Word reveals our entire make-up and reaches every molecule of our being. "***For the Word of God is alive and powerful, and sharper than any two-edged sword, piercing even to the division of soul and spirit, and of joints and marrow, and is a discerner of the thoughts and intents of the heart."*** Hebrews 4:12. As you can see, the Word of God is alive, powerful, sharp, it pierces, divides the spirit from the soul and joints, bone marrow, in-depth thoughts and deep intentions. WOW!

In other words, all three aspects of man are completely covered. ***"The spirit of man is the candle of the Lord searching all the inward parts of the belly."*** Proverbs 20:27. The day we confess Jesus as Lord, our spirit becomes rekindled, lit and reawakened so that we can get to know its Source and Sustainer God from a spiritual standpoint because, "***God is a Spirit…:*** John 4:24.

The infusion of His Word into our transformed mind enables us to realize our past sins are actually forgiven. This means a refreshing – *renewed*– mental capability is now prevalent. Remember, the old carnal nature was not in sync with God. "***Because the carnal mind is enmity against God; for it is not subject to the law of God, nor indeed can be.***" Romans 8:7. We are now equipped with a right state of mind which is capable of knowing God by each of us individually and corporately as the body of Christ. Remember, "…***We are all one in***

***Christ.*"** Galatians 3:28. This is why people marvel at our new stance we take for God reflected in a new lifestyle according to His standards. All pieces of the puzzle *–if you will–* can come together to form a more detailed framework and a complete picture. In essence, we are now properly equipped to represent God to the world as ambassadors for Christ and stewards of God. The way all three aspects of our make-up *–**spirit, soul and body**–* relate to repent, born again and saved are as follows:

1st--**Repent** pertains to our **mind** and what we think after we hear God's Word; this is NOT referring to our spirit or our body.
2nd--**Born Again** relates to our **spirit** which every human on earth receives from God at physical birth regardless of ethnicity or gender.
3rd--**Saved:** refers only to our personal **soul**, genetics and make-up; this is the real you; the conscious perceptive part of you that recognizes, interacts and relates daily with others. See page #13.

4th--**Converted:** embodies how **all three**; our spirit, soul and physical body; they are inter-woven to function corporately. It is through acquiring correct spiritual insight into God's Word which will begin to reshape our life if we choose to apply His spiritual principles.

Never before have the content in God's Word been made so plain to see and easy to understand. Only God's Word separates all aspects of our being so that we can learn of them individually. Because of His brilliance, He brings it all back together so that we can learn them corporately. How profound!

This life on earth is the training ground to prepare us to rule and reign but it is also designed to equip us to judge angels, the world and the twelve tribes of Israel back on earth. "…***and has made us kings and priests to His God and Father.***" Revelations 1:6. "***Do you not know that we shall judge angels? How much more, things that pertain to this life?***" 1 Corinthians 6:3. Hallelujah!

Again, as highly elected officials called ambassadors for Christ and stewards of God on earth, there are important takeaways we hope you embrace. First, we hope you are more familiar with your make-up by knowing your eternal date *–the day you confess Jesus as Lord–* and time. Why? There was a great celebration which took place in Heaven at the time of your second/new birth." ***Likewise, I say unto you, there is joy in the presence of the angels of God over one sinner that repents***." Luke 15:10. This was just like the celebration which took place in the home or hospital when your parents cherished your physical birth. In other words, there is a specific date written in Heaven about you. When ministering to others, it is imperative you know this date as a point of reference for testimonial purposes.

Could you imagine ministering to someone about Christ and your new salvation experience with God and they asked you; when did you decide to give your life to Christ? Your answer, one day I just decided! Or, there was no specific time that I actually recall; I just started going to church regularly. As a representative of God, you want your answer to stand out and to be impactful. Every product made by man has either a date of production and/or, where it was made. It may also contain an expiration date. Manufacturers almost always stamp dates on their important product so they are able to track the progress, use, service, location and person by whom it was assembled.

To take it a step further, what if someone did not know the date they were married? How about their child's DOB? How about when they started their career or when they graduated? What if you forgot their best friend's birth date, their spouse's anniversary or their brother or sister's birth date?

The two primary reasons we are placing such a high importance on the date of confession is; it is the only **eternal date** recorded by God in the universe. This is why there are several 'books' mentioned in the 'The Book of Revelation.' **"*...and the books were opened: and another book was opened, which is the book of life.*"** Rev. 20:12.

Finally, this condensed information is a great way for believers to personally measure their progress, the souls they led to Christ and their annual growth; remember, God is keeping records. God desires all of us to be effective ministers and become a good 'fisher of men.' "***And Jesus said unto them, come follow me, and I will make you to become fishers of men***." Mark 1:17. Finally, "***the fruit of the righteous is a tree of life; and he that win souls is wise***." Proverbs 11:30. This is our Godly directive and personal assignment!

Individual Review or Class Discussion

1—Please write out what being **converted** means to you?

2—We primarily see our physical composition as a physical body; God sees it as a:

3—Please write-out all four (4) aspects of salvation and what role the three (3) parts of your composition applies?

4— Please complete the following: "***There is joy in the presence of the angels of God*** ______

Luke 15:10

5—The natural person is not able to discern or understand God's Word unless their spirit is:

6—Marriage was designed by God; in this book, **M.A.R.R.I.A.G.E** is spelled-out as:

M A R R

I A G E

7—What are two (2) detriments to someone's physical body if they take communion unworthily/not saved?

Chapter V----------→ The Parable of the Word

One of the most detailed and enlightening teachings Jesus provided for His disciples approximately 2,000 years' ago *–and relevant for stewards today–* is 'the parable of The Word.' These twenty verses are filled with insight into the spirit realm as well as the behind the scene occurrences when someone hears God's Word for the first time. According to Scripture, the spiritual world is more real than the physical world in which we live. The reason is that God dwells and operates there; so does our adversary. Also, let's keep in mind that the physical world we see was made by God whom we don't see! "***For He is the Maker of all things***." Jeremiah 10:16. Jesus' parable unveils the following:

<u>The Text</u>: Mark 4:1-20

1-And He –Jesus– began again to teach by the sea side: and there was gathered unto Him a great multitude, so that He entered into a ship, and sat in the sea; and the whole multitude was by the sea on the land.

2 And He taught them many things by parables, and said unto them in His Doctrine,

3 Hearken; Behold, there went out a sower to sow:

4 And it came to pass, as he sowed, some fell by <u>the way side</u>, and the fowls of the air came and devoured it up.

5 And some fell on <u>stony ground</u>, where it had not much earth; and immediately it sprang up, because it had no depth of earth:

6 But when the sun was up, it was scorched; and because it had no root, it withered away.

7 And some <u>fell among thorns</u>, and the thorns grew up, and choked it, and it yielded no fruit.

8 And other fell on good ground, and did yield fruit that sprang up and increased; and brought forth, some thirty, and some sixty, and some an hundred.

9 And He said unto them, he that hath ears to hear, let him hear.

10 And when He was alone, they that were about Him with the twelve asked of Him the parable.

11 And He said unto them, unto you it is given to know the mystery of the kingdom of God: but unto them that are without, all these things are done in parables:

12 That seeing they may see, and not perceive; and hearing they may hear, and not understand; lest at any time they should be converted, and their sins should be forgiven them.

13 And He said unto them, know do you not this parable? and how then will you know all parables?

Jesus' Explanation

14 The sower sows The Word.

15 And these are they by the way side, where the word is sown; but when they have heard, Satan cometh immediately, and taketh away the word that was sown in their hearts.

16 And these are they likewise which are sown on stony ground; who, when they have heard the word, immediately receive it with gladness;

17 And have no root in themselves, and so endure but for a time: afterward, when affliction or persecution arises for the word's sake, immediately they are offended.

18 And these are they which are sown among thorns; such as hear the word,

19 And the cares of this world, and the deceitfulness of riches, and the lusts of other things entering in, choke the word, and it becomes

unfruitful. 20 And these are they which are sown on good ground; such as hear the word, and receive it, and bring forth fruit, some thirtyfold, some sixty, and some an hundred." Mark 4:1-20.

As you have read, there are four examples given yet, only one yielded fruit. Next, why is that so? Is this particular parable critical to know, learn and is it relevant today? Is verse thirteen pointing out to us, if we do not understand this parable, do NOT even attempt to figure out any of the others? Precisely!

Again, why was it only twenty-five (25%) of the hearers bore edible fruit even though they all heard the same message? Beloved, we are going to show Jesus' four (4) examples in a slightly different light so that you will be able to easily identify what will occur in a person's life as you minister. Preparation and insight are great remedies for effective ministry. Now let us see which of the four you identified with.

1st--Are you the person referenced in verse 15? ***'When they have heard, satan cometh immediately, and taketh away the word that was sown in your heart****/subconscious mind?*

2nd—Were you the one detailed in verse 16, ***'where the word was sown on stony ground; who, when they have heard the word, immediately receive it with gladness; but 'have no root in yourself, and so endure but for a time: afterward, when affliction or persecution arises for the word's sake, immediately you get offended?***

3rd—How about this example in verses 18-19; did/will it apply to you? ***'And these are they which are sown among thorns; such as hear the word, 19 And the cares of this world, and the deceitfulness of riches, and the lusts of other things entering in, choke the word, and it becomes unfruitful. Cares, riches or things.'***

4rd—Finally, are you the ardent seeker of truth in verse twenty such as, ***'hear the word, and receive it, and bring forth fruit, some thirtyfold, some sixty, and some one hundred fold?'***

It is enlightening to point out that our enemy only shows up personally for **one** event; **The Kingdom message**. And, his primary goal is to try and steal the most priceless treasure which are keys of the kingdom dynamics. Why, they provide humans with access which allows them to see, recognize and exercise their delegated authority over his works. This includes authority over demons, personal situations, sickness and disease. The enemy is not concerned about us worshipping God, preaching, praying, being good, the blood, Heaven, healing or miracles but primarily God's governance which is now available to humans.

Again, the first thing the enemy does is show up IMMEDIATELY to try and steal our most prized gem. –**verse 15**– We want to reaffirm all of Jesus' parables as substantive, true and accurate and are not ~~stories~~! As we stated in the beginning of this book, a **story** is a fairy-tale and fiction. Remember, God-in-the-flesh –**Jesus**– was only about real life events, exposing the unseen realm, detailing situations and the unveiling of actual conditions which were never made known to man.

Now we know God's Word provides us with **t**eachings, **e**xamples, **a**ccounts and **m**essages. Using the first letters of the four words spells another word, **TEAM.** We are to team–up with God by believing His Word so that we can have exponential effects as confirmed in Scripture. "***How should one chase a thousand, and two put ten thousand to flight***..."Deuteronomy 32:30.

Before we move even deeper into this most stunning parable, let's take a step back and set the precedence early by providing definitions of a small but monumental word, **heart.** By doing so, it will place all of us on the same page of understanding so we can stand together collectively.

One of the most widely used and misappropriated words is 'heart' which Jesus used in verse 15. When the Scripture mentioned '**heart**,' it is **NOT** referring to that vessel in your chest cavity which pumps blood in veins, arteries and capillaries through-out your entire body. It is only referencing someone's mind; actually it is their ***subconscious mind***. As you know, our subconscious mind is the enemy's primary target to try and influence because it will control all immediate and future actions we take! According to Jesus, this is where the Word of God is first planted and begins to take roots. By disclosing this truth, He is preparing us well in advance for exactly what will happen when anyone hears His Word which is what He spells out in verse fifteen.

Our transformed mind is the key to knowledge, memory and all actions toward just about everything in life. You will hear believers say things like, I love God with all my **heart**," or, man's heart is wicked and then place their hand over the left side of their chest cavity. Again, this subtle deception to try and show separation between their heart and their mind. **There is no separation according to God's word!** Please refer to the detailed diagram on page #13.

Beloved, our 'heart' is also related to our conscience. Our heart/mind and conscience are all inter-related through the three pounds of fatty tissue between our ears called our **brain**. God highly values and desires us to fill our mind to capacity. This is why He says, "t***hat you might be filled with all the fullness of God."*** Ephesians 3:19. When we fill our mind with God's Word and choose to believe it, He says the possibilities are endless.

We would like to provide you the most effective solution to get the Word of God fixed and secured in your subconscious mind. It is through meditation of His Word. ***"Meditate upon these things; give thyself wholly to them; that thy profiting may appear to all."*** I Timothy 4:15. See Ps.1:1-3. God is providing critical insight into this magnificent component called your heart *–or subconscious mind–* to you today. This is so that you become more aware of its potent capabilities and unlimited functions. To support meditation, we are to "***Trust in The Lord with all your heart and lean not to your own understanding. In all your ways acknowledge Him and He shall direct your paths.*** Proverbs 3:5-6. As we continue to acknowledge God, He can direct our paths daily.

Individual Review or Class Discussion

1—Please list several things which the "**parable** of the Word" reveals.

2—What is the enemy's action toward new believers when they hear or embrace the message of the kingdom?

3—Which of the four (4) examples in the **Parable of The Word** are you going to embrace? Also, do you know someone who fits any of the other three descriptions?

4—Please complete Mark 9:23. "***But with God all***

5—Please complete I Tim 4:15. "***Meditate upon these things, give***

6—Proverbs 3:5 says, "***Trust in The Lord with***

Verse 6 says, ***"In all your ways acknowledge***

7—When the true **Word/Kingdom of God** is proclaimed, how long does it take the enemy to show-up to try to steal it?

Chapter VI--------→ *Spoken Words and Their Effect*

Beloved, there is a book in the Old Treaty in which very few ministers today share the same view. In fact, there is misunderstanding and mass confusion. This particular book starts-out by giving us great spiritual insight as well as physical facts. Almost immediately, a peaceful situation quickly turns into great suffering, murder of innocent children, slaying of servants, loss of a business and extermination of livestock.

However, later on it concludes with this person owning twice as much as he had before. Let us first ask some detailed questions before we begin to clear up some monumental **mis**understandings! We are making reference to a man who had a book named after him called **Job**. If you have recently read this book, please answer the following seven (**7**) questions before moving forward.

On the other hand, if you have never done so, please familiarize yourself with his situation; or, take a few minutes to read at least the first six chapters to acquaint yourself with his spiritual *–**un**seen–* and physical *–seen–* situation. Enclosed are the interesting questions:

1. What was the very first thing which came to mind when you heard **Job** *–in the Old Testament–* mentioned? ____________________

2. Can God be tempted with evil? Does God allow sickness, disease and death of innocent children to come to your family today in order to prove faithfulness to Him?

3. Can the devil do what he wants or, is he **always** governed by spiritual laws? ____________________________________

4. Job said, "***Though he slays me, yet will I trust in him...***" Job 13:15. To whom was he referring? ____________________________

5. After Job reviewed his personal devastation, what was the final conclusion to which he arrived? ______________________________

6. Did **fear** play any role as to **why** any or all the tragedies occurred?

7. What did God, Job, and the writer conclude about him and his terrible situation? ____

Beloved, we are about to scripturally analyze and carefully review Job's entire situation. This way we can address all you may have heard/thought about him. However, all seven **(7)** questions *–above–* will be answered but **not** in numerical order. Let us first answer question #2 which is about God 'being tempted.' "***Let no one say when he is tempted, "I am tempted by God"; for God cannot be tempted by evil, nor does He Himself tempt anyone.***" James 1:13. This is a major eye-opening Scripture and should put a huge dent in the temptation by God theory you may have heard! God's Holy Spirit has just revealed to us that God **CANNOT** be tempted!

As a great starting point, let's read what God initially mentioned to the enemy. "***Then the LORD said to Satan, "Have you considered My Servant Job, that there is none like him on the earth, a blameless and upright man, one who fears God and shuns evil?"*** Job 1:8.

"***Then the adversary answered the Lord, saying, "has Job feared God for nothing? Have You not made a hedge around him, around his household, and around all that he has on every side? You have blessed the work of his hands, and his possessions have increased in the land. But stretch out Your hand now, and touch all that he has, and he will curse You to Your face.***" Job 1:9-11.

From these verses, the majority of ministers and believers conclude that God is about to allow Job's faithfulness to be tested. However, very few consider or ask why, or why does it seem God allowed this tragedy to occur? The unveiling of Job's terrible situation is that he brought the entire calamity on himself. Let us prove it! Job himself told us in specific detail why the murder of his children, servants, fire and the loss of his business occurred? Job said, "***For the thing I greatly feared has come upon me, and what I dreaded has happened to me.***" Job 3:25. This answers question #6 above. Both fear and torment are clearly evident in his life as well as in these verses.

Did you know in verse twenty-six Job said, "***I am not at ease, nor am I quiet; I have no rest, for trouble comes?*** Job 3:26. It makes you wonder about those who erroneously teach about Job's turmoil. Also, why was this verse not mentioned when ministers taught about Job? Let us provide further evidence that it was Job who chose to open the door for the enemy to inflict him and not God. Please answer the following pinpointed question. Did the tragedies occur first, or was Job living in a life of fear before all the massacre occurred?

Since it is clear that Job was living in fear, this means that He violated a spiritual law which was to embrace fear; this further confirms question #2 above. One of the first things we must understand is that the enemy is **ALWAYS** governed by spiritual laws; he **CANNOT** do what he pleases! This answers question #3 on page 87. Finally, if God and humans are governed by spiritual laws, don't you think the enemy must adhere as well?

God's Unveiling about Job

As enlightened citizens in God's administration today, what we know about God is that He tells us what He sees, NOT what He's looking at; this is not a play on words. Let us provide compelling evidence and relevant examples for you. First, there is Moses; did you know he tried to shun his responsibility of delivering the children of Israel out of bondage when God gave him a directive? He asked God to use his brother Aaron because he was a better speaker and did not stutter.

"***And Moses said unto the LORD, O my Lord, I am not eloquent, neither heretofore, nor since thou hast spoken unto thy servant: but I am slow of speech, and of a slow tongue.***" Exodus 4:10. Then, there is David who was a murderer, conniver and filled with lust; what did God call him? God said he was "***a man after My own heart.***" Acts 13:22. What about Gideon who was a military leader, judge and prophet? Did you know he was afraid of everything? However, what did God say about him? God called him "***mighty man of valor.***" Judges 6:12.

Now, let's go back to Job; when God and the enemy had the initial conversation, God spoke only positive affirmations to the devil about Job. As we know, parents *–including God–* do not speak negatively about His offspring to strangers especially in public. However, when parents speak to their children in private, the details are spelled out on an entirely different platform, isn't that true?

A little later, we will provide precise confirmation when God spoke to Job privately. For now, let us be completely transparent about Job's entire situation so that you will see the whole picture and obtain a correct spiritual insight, moving forward. Let us examine five powerful and detailed statements made by Job himself:

1. Again, ***"For the thing I greatly feared has come upon me, and what I dreaded has happened to me. I am not at ease, nor am I quiet; I have no rest, for trouble comes."*** Job 3:25-26. In other words, he was living in torment.

2. After that he said, "***Teach me, and I will hold my tongue: and cause me to understand wherein I have erred.***" Job 6:24. How would this statement hold up if he were in a court of law? This verse clearly spells out that Job convicted himself for all that occurred! In other words, Job just sentenced himself! Also, it answers question #5. And, in chapter six verse twenty-five says, "***How forcible are right words***!"

3. Did you know Job himself stated, "***I have sinned***?" Job 7:20.

4. Now, let's take a look at what the writer stated about Job. "***Job hath spoken without knowledge and his words were without wisdom.***" Job 34:35. Why would the writer of Job make such a bizarre statement if it were not true?

5. Then, the writer went even further, "***Therefore Job opens his mouth in vain; He multiplies words without knowledge.*** "Job 35:16. What, let's read that again!

6. Now, let us read God's one–on–one private chat with Job we touched on earlier. "***Then the LORD answered Job out of the whirlwind, and said, "who is this that darkens counsel by words without knowledge?***" Job 38:1-2. This answers #7 Pg. 88

After we carefully review these six stunning facts mentioned above, we are to **re**consider all the teachings and things we have heard about Job. The evidence is all around that it was his ignorance which opened all the doors to destruction; it was not a test by God but the use of wrong words, ignorance and fear which caused destruction. "***My people are destroyed for lack of knowledge...***" Hosea 4:6.

Thinking Rationally & With Clear Evidence!

If we think logically about Job's sickness and consider that by him being sick brings glory to God, then he should ask for **more** sickness, right! Today, if we believe God is testing us, then we should **not** ask for prayer, advice or go to our doctor or hospital for a remedy, MRI or take medication.

When we embrace sickness, neglect exercise and have bad health they embarrass God, not bring Him glory. This is why Jesus came. And, the Scripture says, "***...I have come that they may have life, and that they may have it more abundantly***. John 10:10. Also, "***beloved, I pray that you may prosper in all things and be in health, just as your soul prospers.***" III John 2. Finally, "***...and I will take sickness away from the midst of thee.***" Exodus 23:25.

Now let us state what we know about our Heavenly Father and what He says about fear. First, we know, "***For God has not given us a spirit of fear, but of power and of love and of a sound mind***." II Timothy 1:7. Notice in the New Treaty **power, love** and a **sound mind** are co-workers from God to ensure wholeness. Soundness of mind – *without fear*– brings about confidence, assurance and informs us to take positive action. On the other hand, fear will cause us to speak negatively, act fearful and be apprehensive in the things we do. Therefore, when we carefully re–examine the book of Job, take the information in the New Treaty as supporting evidence for additional considerations, several points should immediately jump out at us.

First, Job had no clue that there was an enemy called satan; neither did Job mention or blame him for bringing sores and boils on his body. Remember, Job said, "***Though He slay me, yet will I trust Him***..." Job 1:15. Who was Job referencing? He thought God was slaying him, not the enemy! This answers question #4 on page 87. It is true Job made this statement, but what he said was **not** a true statement. Beloved, as we know, Our Manual of Life says, "***God is love.***" 1 John 4:8. "***God is just.***" 1 Samuel 45:21. "***God is righteous.***" Lamentations 1:18 Again, "***Let no one say when he is tempted, "I am tempted by God"; for God cannot be tempted by evil, nor does He Himself tempt anyone.***" James 1:13. These are the facts!

Therefore, the evidence is crystal clear that God was NOT testing Job to prove anything to the devil. How about another pinpointed question? Why would God allow the enemy to kill precious children, hard-working servants and innocent animals just to appease the enemy? It does not make any sense! This would be like a criminal asking a righteous judge for permission to kill his grandchildren; burn down their son's business, inflict his only son with disease and impose pain on him who is a law-abiding citizen just to prove a point.

God is not subject to any of the devil's whim, influence, or appeals concerning any of His seven billion offspring, not one! Please do not allow anyone's teaching or opinions to sway you from clear evidence presented but flush all contrary teachings down the toilet! **The book of Job is primarily about the spiritual realm, spoken words, and danger of embracing fear whose partner is torment.** It is not about suffering, testing or enduring sickness to bring God glory. We know the devil is a spirit being and must **always** wait for spiritual laws – *question #3*– to be violated before he can begin to act; again, he **cannot** do as he wants; He is **NOT** God!

Even in our natural world, laws must always be violated before consequences can occur. Let us prove it to you. What if a police officer comes to you tomorrow and says, "you are under arrest!" What would be your response? I think your answer would be a sequence of one–to–five words like: "**why, what have I done?**" You see, we know that all things are governed by laws. God Himself is governed by His own words which He firmly upholds and stands by! It is for this reason God said, "***I watch over My word to perform it.***" Jeremiah 1:12. In other words, I Am looking where My Word is being used so that I can assist in what was stated!

Defining Fear, it's Effect & Torment!

One U.S. Vice President, Henry Wallace *–who served in office from 1941-1945–* made a relevant and noteworthy statement about fear. He said, "**the source of all our mistakes is fear**." Have you ever greatly feared something or someone? Do you remember how it made you feel every day? Or, do you presently fear something or someone? Fear will destroy your life, your family's and negatively impact those around you. As you know, the effects of fear can, at times, lead someone to commit suicide. Fear is very terrifying and it can stay with us indefinitely if we do not obtain spiritual truth from God's Word or know how to counter its destructive nature. Let us address and define fear so that we will all be on the same page of understanding.

This is necessary so that you will easily recognize fear when it knocks at your door or shows-up. **Fear** is a feeling induced by perceived danger. And, it is something bad which you do not wish to happen but subconsciously think can occur. This is exactly what Job experienced. Again, fear always comes on the scene through violation and brings its partner called torment. For example, if you fear a person, you will not go where you think they are; you will avoid, change direction, adjust your habits, make mistakes, do things you would not ordinarily do, or run and hide.

An acronym which I heard years ago which accurately pinpoints fear is: **F**alse, **E**vidence **A**ppearing, **R**eal. Again, fear is always accompanied with **torment** which can keep us up all night and without needed rest as it was with Job. Also, it interferes with our thought process. Remember, this was exactly what Job told us that torment was doing to him. He said, "...***I have no rest, for trouble comes.***" Job 3:26. We know sleepless nights have devastating effects on our mental state and can physically paralyze our brilliant capabilities. Also, we know insomnia is NOT from God because His

Word says, "*…for so He gives his beloved sleep*." Psalms 127:2. What about fear? "***God has NOT given us a spirit of fear, but of power and of love and of a sound mind."*** 2 Timothy 1:7. As you can clearly see, God desires all His offspring to get restful sleep! Today, torment is defined **as a severe physical or mental suffering and to worry or to annoy excessively**. Most people like to blame the enemy for things when in reality he has nothing to do with the situation; the problem stems from us choosing to clutch things we were not built to carry-around.

Do you remember Shakespeare's perspective about man? "*The fault lies not in the stars but in ourselves*." Today this is not accepted as true by the majority of believers because Job's suffering has been erroneously taught which is why people have blamed God for generations. The real reason 'WHY' the tragedies occur is rarely addressed accurately.

One final question; **who was the guilty party in the tragic account of Job?** Was it God, the devil or Job who initiated the process? In fact, Job himself Job told us, "***I have sinned***?" Job 7:20. Beloved, from now on, we should always consider all the facts and evidence presented *–like investigators, jurors and judges–* before arriving at any conclusion in all we read. Even our judicial system weighs all evidence presented before sentencing. Did you know, even if Job knew about satan, he would not be capable of handling him? The distribution of power and personal authority was given only to New Testament saints by Jesus the Christ, not to any saint including Moses.

We are the privileged ones! The majority of Old Treaty saints were in the dark about the spirit realm; neither were they given any jurisdiction over evil. This is why God had to come personally to lead by example in the man, Jesus Christ. Therefore, power and authority was only given to converts by Jesus in the New Covenant. He said, "***Behold, I give unto you power to tread on serpents and scorpions, and over all the power of the enemy: and nothing shall by any means hurt you***." Luke 10:19. Now we know that this statement was NEVER made to anyone in the Old Covenant. Also, "***You shall receive power after the Holy Spirit has come upon you***." Acts 1:8. Job's ignorance of how spoken words are to be used coupled with his unseen house guests of fear and torment kept the door open for satanic spirits to come–and–go as they pleased. Think back for a moment, how many times have you heard 'fear' mentioned as the key component of destruction when ministers taught about Job?

Most Ministers' Answer to Job's Turmoil

Over a period of several years, I inquired of many prominent ministers, citizens and lay-persons as to why those terrible things happened to Job. One minister mentioned that the entire church body is divided based on Job's situation. He went on to say, some believe God allows tragedies to show the devil that Job was faithful. Another minister's response about Job's turmoil was, "it was like a side bet between God and the devil."

On my quest to diligently find out more perceived thoughts surrounding Job's turmoil, I asked this question. **Did Job fear first, or did the tragedies occur first?** One minister looked at me stunned and stated, 'I don't know.' Needless to say, I did not respond. I asked many other minister, why did those tragedies happen to Job? They provided the most common answer which in excess of 90% of ministers gave; 'it was to show the devil Job would continue serving him regardless of what he was going through.' Probably the most interesting of all answers I received was from a newly appointed pastor who told me that God was testing them to suffer and go through the same things like Job. This answers question #1 on page # 87.

In my pursuit, there was only one minister in Concord, NC who mentioned the root cause was fear. The final tally remained: over 90% of ministers mentioned it was some form of a test by God. It is critical to mention that Old Covenant teachings provided hope, prophecies and historical examples we are to learn about and become familiar. However, they are not to be used primarily as doctrine nor spiritual application today. Since Jesus –**God in the flesh**– we are provided with a better covenant *–see Hebrews 8:6–* with much more details about mankind and the spirit realm. We know Jesus lived here physically for thirty-three and a half years and exposed believers to the spiritual world and their authority. Then, He showed us exactly how to be effective using His matchless name. Jesus is the premier

standard to live by and not uphold man's theology or the Old Testament examples. This means, whatever is written in the Old Treaty must be weighed and measured by Jesus' words, teachings and the New Treaty's promises which takes precedence. By this I mean, if Jesus says one thing about a particular subject and anyone says something different; who are we to follow? As stewards, we are to vie for all of Jesus' teaching as accurate, true, insightful and the highest standard! Often-times Jesus said, "you have heard it said..." **but I say**..." Jesus was teaching some things contrary to what was vigorously held as law and traditions of men!
When we take time to carefully re-examine the book of Job and ask the Holy Spirit to unveil the truth, He will disclose relevant and accurate information. "***If so be that you have heard him, and have been taught by him, as the truth is in Jesus***..." Ephesians 4:21. Without Jesus, there is no: **R**ighteousness, **E**ternal-life, **V**ision, **E**mpowerment, **L**ove, **A**uthority, **T**ruth, **I**nstructor, **O**utpouring, or **N**ewness. These attributes spell the word '**REVELATION**.' Going back to fear, according to the New and Better Covenant, "***there is no fear in love; but perfect love casts out fear, because fear*** *–has–* ***involves torment. But he who fears has not been made perfect in love."*** 1 John 4:18.

God **CANNOT** be tempted; He does **NOT** work with the devil. And, God **NEVER** allows bad things to come to His own blood bought children today. Even in the Old Treaty it says. ***"...no good thing will He withhold from those who walk uprightly***." Psalms 84:11. Please note, fear is more about the unknown and less of what we perceive to be true. We bring things on ourselves *–like children do–* through their own ignorance of the laws of how the spirit world functions. Therefore, the Scripture says, "***Study to show yourself approved by God, a workman who need not be ashamed, rightly dividing the word of truth***. II Timothy 2:15. If we study, we will get the right answers.

Solution and Relevant Examples

As ambassadors for Christ today, we have God's entire Library of sixty-six books and heightened spiritual senses in dealing with adverse activities. "***For we are not ignorant of his devices***." II Corinthians 2:11. This statement was NOT made to anyone in the Old

Treaty. As we mentioned, they all had a very limited spiritual understanding and insight of the spirit world. Elisha was one of the few prominent prophets who was aware of God's spiritual invisible **army** in his midst. II Kings 6:17. What about Daniel the Prophet? Please read ***Daniel 10:1-13.*** Was he aware of what was taking place behind the scenes while he was praying and fasting for twenty-one days? No, he was not! How do we know this? When the angel finally came to him, the angel explained all the spiritual activities from the 1st to the 21st day. We can extract from Daniel's situation that he too was **NOT** made aware of any spiritual battles which were taking place in the Heavenly realm. Today, it's different; we have both the benefit of Old Testament saint's perseverance as well as Jesus' New Treaty promises and delegated authority.

The rights given us spiritually since the time of Jesus is just like what is deputized to police officers. This same right is provided to believers the minute they confess Jesus as Lord. See Romans 10:9-10. As Offspring of God, we know, "***If others be partakers of this power over you, are not we rather? Nevertheless, we have not used this –*** authority– ***power; but suffer all things, lest we should hinder the gospel of Christ."*** 1 Corinthians 9:12. This is only referencing the accessible power of the Holy Spirit who gives us both the insight and authority.

We are the only ones who have been given this authority over the enemy, not **any** of the Old Testament saints, not one! If we are troubled with fear and timidity, it will only escalate and bring its partners of torment into our home, circumstance, business and cause separation within the family unit. If there exists an ounce of fear in us, we are to speak directly to the circumstance today by first confessing it immediately to our Source and Father who is God; in Jesus' name. We are to come confidently and say:

- *Abba, Father in the name of Jesus the Christ, You said I have a right to come to You. I confess to You that I have been disobedient. You said, I am to cast all my cares upon you for you care for me."* 1 Peter 5:7. *I am sorry I have been disobedient by embracing the fear of (* ... ...) but I will no longer carry it because it is heavy and has been*

> *tormenting me.* ***(See 1 John 4:18.)****. Thank you Father I have done according to what You have said I am to do about fear or anything else which tries to take up residence in Your temple –my body– or in my transformed mind in the name of Jesus. Thank you Lord I have done what you said to do about fear. I am strong and have confidence in You!*

After concluding the above petition, if or when contrary thoughts or adverse feelings of fear arise, begin to verbally express a praise of thanksgiving for the victory over those fears. If not, they will interfere with your relationship with the Holy Spirit. In the Book of the Revelation of Jesus Christ, it states how believers will be able to successfully overcome adversity. It says, "***And they overcame him by the blood of the Lamb and by the word of their testimony***." Revelations 12:11. Even though this is for believers in the future, it can be applied for us today.

As offspring, you are to use your words to serve you and lift up others; not bring them down! Also, it is essential you write down the date, time of your prayer and commitment to the Lord. This is simply as a point of reference, so you can confidently revert to it just in case you should ever begin to doubt. You are free! Remember the Scripture says, "***Cast not away therefore your confidence, which hath great recompense of reward***." Hebrews 10:35. As a reminder, "I was set free on (the date of __/__/20__). By doing so, we are establishing roots of confidence in ourselves and assurance of continued victory in Christ. The confession –above– you make will attach itself to you, your home and personal situation so you will have peace, going forward.

One hot summer day, I was speaking to a preacher about the book of Job and the root cause of his pain, death of his children and suffering. I went on to explain that the reason all those tragedies occurred was because Job embraced fear. This minister assertively asked, "why are you telling me this Paul?" I mentioned it was because of the erroneous teaching about Job's situation. This preacher became very quiet on the phone and in a very low tone mentioned the following. "I have lived in fear all my life and lost my family, my business and my home because of fear. What a stunning unveiling! This was an eye-opening experience for me as well! He concluded that he had never told this to anyone before! We proceeded and agreed in prayer; I rebuked that foul spirit and he thanked me for both the new insight of Job's situation as well as the remedy to his own life's circumstances. After praying for him, I gave him the date and time as a point of reference. Again, this reference point was to secure the new foundation built on truth. Finally, it served as a reminder that God had just delivered him from the years of deception and bondage brought on by fear.

Exposing Truth about the Spirit World

Beloved, **if** our enemy can do what he wants whenever he wants, we are all in deep trouble. And, we would be guaranteed to lose every time because we can't see him. Therefore, we would not know when he's coming or the direction he is approaching. In other words, we would always be caught off guard. Some people in the U.S. have seen the movie "Predator" starring Arnold Schwarzenegger and Carl Weathers which took place in the jungle of Central America. This alien/predator was able to kill humans at his discretion because they could not see him. I don't know about you beloved, but I don't like to lose. And, I don't want to fight against something I cannot see.

You may be up to the challenge, but I prefer to know what I'm up against. If we are going to fight against someone we can't see, then we should acquire as much available information as possible from our Father's manual to ensure success. This way, we would not fail, wouldn't you agree? Even though "Predator" was a science fiction movie, it exemplifies what could happen to us as children of God if we are not properly equipped and informed about the spiritual world in our midst.

Again, "***we are not ignorant of his*** *–devices–* ***schemes.*** II Corinthians 2:11. Keep in mind, God has given us keys to lock out or allow things in both the natural and spirit realm. "***And I will give you the keys of the kingdom of heaven, and whatever you bind on earth will be bound in heaven, and whatever you loose on earth will be loosed in heaven.***" Matthew 16:19. This means we hold the 'key' to why things happen. Two critical things just happened; God has now opened our eyes and given us keys into the spirit realm. The **only** way we are to believe that God allowed the tragedies of Job to occur to prove a point to the enemy, is **IF** we deleted chapters 3:25-26, 6:24-25, 7:20, 34:35, 35:16 and 38:1-2. Then, we could conclude that God was working with the enemy through no fault of Job, which is **ridiculous**!

Individual Review or Class Discussion

1—What did this description of ***Job*** reveal or mean to you?

2—Did **fear**, **torment** and **no rest** impact Job's life? Please explain.

3—Is there a difference between how God worked in the Old Treaty and the way He works in the New Testament?

4—What did our longest reigning vice-president say about **fear**? Also, can the enemy do what he wants when he wants?

5—What are three (3) things Job himself said about his situation?

6—Were the Old Testament saints aware of the devil and/or spiritual activity in their midst? Also, please state your findings.

Chapter VII--------→ Jesus, the Author and Example of Effective Word Usage.

In this day and age, we should be on heightened alert and become more conscious that there are effects associated with all our dispelled words whether we mean what we say or not. The Word of Life says, "***jesting is sin***." Ephesians 5:4. As we previously mentioned, there is an even greater effect when we include God's Word in conjunction with our own. Unseen forces await each expressed word we utter as it was during Jesus' ministry and all the Apostles as well.

"***Or do you think that I cannot now pray to My Father, and He will provide Me with more than twelve legions of angels?***" Matthew 12:53. Just because we do not see angels does not mean they are not accessible and are presently working every day on our behalf. Jesus constantly disclosed that He was in spiritual battles and words were the instruments He used. This is the reason He said, "***For by your words you will be justified, and by your words you will be condemned.***" Matthew 12:37. And "...***every idle word that men shall speak, they shall give account thereof in the day of judgment***." Matthew 12:36.

The Scripture discloses what type of battles we will face on earth and the weapon we are to deploy. "***For the weapons of our warfare are not carnal but mighty in God for pulling down strongholds***." II Corinthians 10:4. Therefore, as a child of the Most-High, whether we are new to the kingdom family or mature in Him, the weapons which are to be used in combat on earth are not knives, guns or bombs, but authoritative verbal words. Words expressed by petitions – *coupled with thanksgiving*– create immediate changes in the spirit realm before the results are ever manifested in the physical. This is awesome and true based on the written evidence in the Word of Truth.

Remember, throughout the temptation of Jesus, He spoke faith filled words as well as those established and written as law. We are to realize we have been given the same degree of authority. The unveiling is that the enemy is jealous of us because we are physical beings who have been adopted into God's spiritual lineage and are able to affect both realms. Our invisible adversary seat is in Germany but the atmospheric invisible realm is where we now have authority to operate. The Word of God discloses, "***For we do not wrestle against flesh and blood, but against principalities, against powers, against the rulers of the darkness of this age, against spiritual hosts of wickedness in the heavenly places.***" Ephesians 6:12. In other words, what we don't see in the natural is real in the spiritual.

I think it would be a great idea for us to come to grips with God's reality and thoroughly convince ourselves of who we are as God's offspring. This is why we are to designate time to meditate and inwardly digest our Father's directives on how to conduct ourselves in this new arena. Again, "***We are not ignorant of his devices***." 2 Corinthians 2:11. It is crystal clear evidence that spoken faith filled words worked for our elder brother Jesus at **all** times. He is our example to pattern our life after and NEVER man's perspective or their new theology. Beloved, did you know there are **two** types of faith and **four** levels in Scripture? Romans 12:3 tells us, there is a measure given to every person. Then, there is another given by the Holy Spirit at His discretion. See I Cor. 12:9. The **four** levels are:

1--Little faith,
2--Faith
3--Great faith
4--Most Holy faith

God's Word says, "***Looking unto Jesus, the author and finisher of our faith*** ..." Hebrews 12:2. Now that we are identified with God, all things should be perceived from a spiritual origin because "***God is spirit***." John 4:24. Therefore, when we speak His words with our mouths, it will affect the real and spirit realm.

Exercising Our Delegated Authority

Today, whenever adverse situations arise, we are to verbally and authoritatively speak to it and begin with, "**it is written**... as Jesus firmly stated. Again, we are to exercise the same type of authority police officers do in the natural world. They pursue, restrict or arrest violators which in our case are spiritual in nature. Remember, our elder brother exercised dominance over demons who had people bound for years in all areas of life. The Scripture tells us: ***"And ought not this woman, being a daughter of Abraham, whom Satan hath bound, lo, these eighteen years..."*** Luke 13:16. Again, "***Study to show yourself approved by God, a workman who need not be ashamed, rightly dividing the word of truth***. II Timothy 2:15. Finally, "***You are of God, little children, and have overcome them: because greater is he that is in you, than he that is in the world.*** I John 4:4. Meditation can provide us with the spiritual adrenaline to support our capabilities. And, God's Word provides us with eye opening promises and exclusive rights to operate in His realm!

Going forward, if we fear or are fearful of something or someone; we are to use our sword by stating, ***"God has not given us a spirit of fear, but of power and of love and of a sound mind."*** 2 Timothy 1:7. Whenever someone is in need, we can confidently say: '***YOUR WORD SAYS' "…my God shall supply all your need according to His riches in glory by Christ Jesus***." Philippians 4:19.

Again, whenever we are tempted we are to say, ***IT IS WRITTEN:*** *'My Lord will not allow anything to confront His child (me) unless He knew I would be able to handle and overcome this situation so He gets the glory.'* 1 Corinthians 10:13 paraphrased. Our words are our sword which we are to deploy and fire like a gun. As we know, '**words'** can be spelled out as a:

W-eapon
O-f
R esource *and*
D-etailed
S-upport o

God's Treaty confirms the magnitude of this acronym. "***Out of the same mouth proceeds blessing and cursing. My brethren, these things ought not so to be. Does a fountain send forth at the same place sweet water and bitter***?" James 3:10-11. And, we know this includes both the spiritual and the natural world. In some cases, we are not even to speak because our words will always create a circumstance. Now let us simply place the letter "S" in front of "word;" you get the word SWORD which we are to use daily. It too spells out another critical word mentioned in Scripture, "***SWORD of the spirit***" Ephesians 6:17 which is the Word of God. It is a:

> **S**-pecial
> **W**-eapon
> **O**-f
> **R**-esource *or*
> **D**-ivision

As we know, a sword divides, pierces, cuts, severs and can be used to kill others by its user. Our sword in the spirit realm is actually prayer not physically devices like guns, knives or bombs. The apostle Luke tells us why we are to familiarize ourselves with the Word of God.

"***For the Word of God is alive and powerful, and sharper than any two-edged sword, piercing even to the division of soul and spirit, and of joints and marrow, and is a discerner of the thoughts and intents of the heart."*** Hebrews 4:12. In today's terminology and from a properly trained soldier's standpoint this verse reveals that we will be working with live ammunition which has devastating effects in both the spiritual realm as well as the natural. He went on to say it requires both familiarization and ongoing training in order for us to maintain a high degree of effectiveness.

As we stated earlier –page 77– this weapon is far superior than anything we will ever handle or be familiar with in this natural world; like a sword, it has razor sharp cutting edges which can separate every aspect of man's composition; the **spirit** from the **soul**, the soul from the **body**, even the things we have not yet **thought** of or **intend to do** cannot be hidden from it. This is simply stunning!

In essence, God's Word is our **sword** in this life. Why would Our Father tell us about this spiritual tool and provide insight if we are not supposed to use it? God desires all His offspring to obtain:

> **Knowledge** which is critical **information**.
> **Understanding** which we know is clear **comprehension**.
> Finally, we are to deploy **Wisdom** which is **application**

God knows all kinds of situations will daily confront His stewards; so He wants us properly equipped and ready to properly address circumstances as they arise. Our Elder Brother exercised and used words as His servant; He spoke to the wind, water, ***see Mark 4:3 7-39,*** trees ***See Matthew 21:19.*** He went on to say we can speak to mountains, ***See Matthew 17:20,*** demons ***See Luke 10:17,*** sickness and disease, ***see Matthew 4:23;*** He raised the dead***, Luke 7:14.*** Just as all of the above obeyed Him, so must they follow suit to His offspring as well. Jesus said, "***most assuredly, I say to you, he who believes in Me, the works that I do he will do also; and greater works than these he will do, because I go to My Father***." John 14:12. Hallelujah!

Words Are to Be Used as Our Servant.

Prior to believing and confessing Jesus as Lord, our everyday words were used exclusively for communicating. However, as a believer, we should now begin to recognize the impact all our words will carry and how God sees us. "…***and raised us up together, and made us sit together in the heavenly places in Christ Jesus***." Ephesians 2:6. When we begin to grasp where we are seated, we should become conscious of both what we say and do!

Jesus' encounter with the Centurion provides us with the perfect example of how words are to be used. Throughout all of Israel, this was the only example where the words "great faith" was used. Now let us examine this detailed situation. ***Now when Jesus had entered Capernaum, a centurion came to Him, pleading with Him, saying, "Lord, my servant is lying at home paralyzed, dreadfully tormented." and Jesus said to him, "I will come and heal him." The centurion answered and said, "Lord, I am not worthy that You should come under my roof. But only speak a word, and my servant will be healed.***

For I also am a man under authority, having soldiers under me. And I say to this one, 'Go,' and he goes; and to another, 'Come,' and he comes; and to my servant, 'Do this,' and he does it." When Jesus heard it, He marveled, and said to those who followed,

"Assuredly, I say to you, I have not found such great faith, not even in Israel!" Matthew 8:5-10. As you can see, the centurion immediately recognized Jesus' authority because he knew Jesus was authorized by Heaven just as he was authorized from Rome. Basically, he was telling Jesus *–regarding his soldiers–*, I say go, and they go; I say come, and they come; I say do this, and they do it. In essence, **my servants obey me in the natural, the same way your words obey you in the spiritual.**

Therefore, I know all you have to do is to speak the words and they will carry out their assignment. In our modern phrase, Jesus would term it as, 'he's got the picture'. Let us look at others who employ the servitude of words today. You can use for example our president, a prime minister, judges, doctors, police officers, managers, teachers, business owners, foreman, executives and true believers today. All of the above, when they know who they are, they will use what they have been given. They no longer use their physical strength or abilities to the extent they did before their assigned position.

Those who recognize early that words carry out most of their assignments will begin to live a far more victorious life than those who don't. They will use words to perform most of their daily functions. In today's business world, a company's financial standing or survival hinges on the words *–decisions–* owners/managers make in order for the corporation, LLC or sole proprietors or partnership to enjoy continued success and profitability in the future.

In the same way as proper words/decisions are critical to prolong a company's existence, God desires His children to use words selectively so they can begin to enjoy the fruit of their lips. This is why reading His Instruction Manual every day is so critical to success, "***A man will be satisfied with good by the fruit of his mouth.***" Proverbs 12:14. Therefore, whenever we are in any adverse situation or a need arises, we are to begin to employ what is spiritual in order to receive what we need in the natural. The Scripture tells stewards and ambassadors for Christ, "***And my God shall supply all your need according to His riches in glory by Christ Jesus.***" Philippians 4:19. God's Word discloses that maturity or completion in Him is evident among those who do not use words to offend others. "*...**if any man***

offend not in word, the same is a perfect man, and able to bridle the whole body. " James 3:2. Proper word usage today is key to living a successful life in God as food is for sustenance of our body. Not only will we be judged for the things we say, but also for any adverse situations which were created by our use of our words. On the other hand, we will be commended for the properly aligned words we used to aid and assist someone towards victory.

The Words We Use to Serve Us, At Times Need a Break

As important as it is for us to understand and use words as our servant, at times listening carefully can be of equal or more importance. To put it bluntly, there are times we should be quiet and simply listen. The Scripture says, "***So then, my beloved brethren, let every man be swift to hear, slow to speak, slow to wrath.***" James 1:19. Whenever we choose to remain quiet, it clearly shows that we are exercising discipline, self-control and humility. Why, because we are now made more aware of the full nature and effect of words.

What we know as self-exaltation leads to pride which is one of the things God hates about humans. And, most people have heard or read that pride always goes before a fall. "***Pride goes before destruction***..." Proverbs 16:18. By adhering to the Word of Truth, we will develop the art of listening. This way, we will be able to properly direct our response to situations where it can cause the greatest effect.

For others who pay little attention to what they hear, it will cause them to be impulsive in their response which shows ignorance of God's Word. This will also expose immaturity in dealing with others. A friend in the financial field once made a comment to me about a client who spent very little time listening to personal counsel and timely advice. As a result, the client eventually suffered a severe setback financially. Disappointed by the outcome of the client's situation, the friend made this statement to me. He said, "that's why God made us with two ears and only one mouth'. How simple, but true this is! Despite the fact everyone knows this to be obvious, very few of us realize the significance. The principle is, we are to listen twice as much as we speak. Even though we can use words to serve ourselves and exalt others, we are to learn to apply God's principle of being swift *–quick–* to hear, and slow to speak, slow to wrath. Therefore, not everything we hear requires our verbal response or any impulsive reaction. By putting into practice the art of listening, it will allow us to respond more appropriately, so that when we do respond, the greatest effect will accompany our situation.

Individual Review or Class Discussion

1—Please complete the following, King Solomon' said "***A man will be satisfied with good***

Prov. 12:14.

2—What are some situations you recall when your words were used to **change, encourage**, **hurt** or **help** someone?

3—Please list the four (4) levels of **faith** mentioned on page 102.

4—Please complete the following Scripture, "***we are to be "***..

James 1:19

5—Are there limitations to our spoken words? Are words eternal?

6—What does the Scripture state of our **words** in Matt. 12:36-37?

7—Please put **wisdom**, **knowledge** and **understanding** in order of process; 1st, 2nd 3rd. Then, use one word to describe each of them.

Chapter VIII------------→ Our Body and Its Role in Salvation and Ministry

The single most often overlooked and negated components when it comes to having a complete relationship with God is our physical body. However, when someone understands just how critical their body is in the whole scope of salvation, they begin treating it as God's prized instrument and not treat it as their own.

The primary focus in this section is to provide clarity of information so that we understand the intricate functions of the clay structure we call the body. And, as most of us would agree, the part of us which we feel most comfortable talking about is our body because it is where our sense of being and character derived its development. Early in life, we learned that our body features five standard physiological functions which are sight, hearing, taste, smell and touch. Again, the familiar place which is used in the living out of these senses on earth is called the body.

The Word of God says it so brilliantly. "***I will praise You, for I am fearfully and wonderfully made; marvelous are Your works, and that my soul knows very well.***" Psalm 139:14. King David realized just how perfect our body was put together. He knew if it was wonderfully made/designed, there had to be a **Designer**! How brilliant those old folks were. Thousands of years later, we are just realizing God's brilliance. Listed below are a few of God's sheer genius spelled out about our body which He designed. There is the skeletal which is made up of two hundred seventy (270) bones at birth and by adulthood some fuse together and end up at two hundred six (206). The skeletal muscles comprise over six hundred fifty (650).

In one day, our blood travels 19,000 km (12,000 miles)—which is four times the distance across the US from coast-to-coast through arteries, capillaries and veins. Our bodies could **not** possibly have evolved because it was meticulously designed and intricately put together by God. For further illustration, we will provide a summary of something we are familiar with and conclude by asking just one related question. Here we go; the average car we drive around or would like to own someday is made up of approximately 30,000 individual parts. Which one of those 30,000 parts do you think is **<u>not</u>** designed for that particular vehicle? Do you see how silly it is to think that our body just happened to come together by chance? This would be like saying the 30,000 parts came together and built your favorite model, features, color, equipment and seats. The acronyms below separate intelligence from theory; as it does **<u>creation</u>** from **<u>evolution</u>**. They are as far apart as the east is from the west. As you are about to read, both words drastically oppose the other which are spelled-out as follows:

C-ognitive	**E**-xcuses
R-easoning	**V**-oid
E-lohim –**God**–	**O**-f
A-ssigned	**L**-ogic
T-o	**U**-sing
I-mpact	**T**-heories &
O-ur	**I**-deologies *to*
N-ature	**O**-ffset
	N-ature

The book of Romans 1:20 epitomizes, explains and capsulizes both terms for us in as little as thirty-five words. It reads, "***For the invisible things of Him from the <u>creation</u> of the world are <u>clearly seen</u>, being understood by the things that are <u>made</u>, even his eternal power and Godhead; so that they are without <u>excuse</u>.***" Even before we can consider evolution, it has to measure up against **design** in order to try and contend with creation. For example, there is a cooking show called, "Beat Bobby Flay." In order to contend with Bobby for the ultimate showdown, two challengers must face–off against each other. The winner then qualifies for a face-off against Bobby Flay. This is the parallel we are using in order to determine or even consider if evolution is indeed a worthy opponent. Design is:

D-etailed &
E-xact
S-ignature of
I-ntelligence &
G-od's
N-otification:

By the way, the '**N**' in DESIGN of the acronym means, a written or printed notice or warning; **God's Word**! Our physical body is of a comprehensive blue-print and a fascinating piece of artwork because the Creator God used Himself, His Son and the Holy Spirit –**The Godhead**– as the blueprint. In God's Instruction Manual it says, "***Then God said, "Let Us make man in Our image, according to Our likeness and let them have dominion…".*** Genesis 1:26. In other words, God was thinking about Himself when He created us because He constructed our bodies to ultimately house His Holy Spirit along with our own spirit. **STUNNING**!

The human body is the most awesome, blessed and sacred place on the planet. It is not weak or feeble but strong and fascinating. God is about to disclose something monumental; He said, "***Flee immorality. Every other sin that a man commits is outside the body, but the immoral man sins against his own body. Or do you not know that your body is a temple of the Holy Spirit who is in you, whom you have from God, and that you are not your own?"*** I Corinthians 6:18. Again, our intent is that all who chooses to sincerely follow Christ will grasp this ENORMOUS truth!

As it is so common today, when most people think of their body, they invariably feel it belongs solely to them for their discretion. They pierce it, color it, alter it, give it illegal drugs, alcohol, make adjustments to it and add to it as they see fit. The fact we all feed, clothe and take care of our bodies daily does not warrant our overwhelming conviction to feel we can do with it as we please. The Word says, "***You shall not make any cuttings in your flesh for the dead, nor tattoo any marks on you: I am the LORD***." Leviticus 19:28. We tattoo our body without realizing it really belongs to someone else.

This would be like painting your neighbor's car or house the color you want. When you gave your life to the Lord, you relinquished all personal rights as well. You cannot give your body to someone else outside of marriage because it's NOT yours! Remember, He no longer dwells in any physical structure made with hands for the last two thousand years. "***…The Most High does not dwell in temples made***

with hands, as the prophet says*:**" Acts 7:48. Before Jesus' ascension back to His Father, He instructed His disciples where to go and who they will receive when they get to the upper room in the city of Jerusalem. "for you are the temple of the living God; as God has said, I will dwell in them, and walk in them; and I will be their God, and they shall be my people.***" II Corinthians 6:16.

The Making of the –House– Body

To understand in much greater detail how God constructed the human body, let us revert once again to the architect and manufacturer whose address is Genesis 2:7. As you have previously read, "***and the LORD God formed man of the dust of the ground, and breathed into his nostrils the breath of life; and man became a living soul***." Genesis 2:7. Let us now visualize this sequence slowly. From the dirt of the ground mixed with water *–clay–*, God formed a figure or statue.

Through recent research, up to 60% of the human adult body is water. According to H.H. Mitchell, Journal of Biological Chemistry 158, the brain and physical heart are composed of 73% water and the lungs are about 83% water. The skin contains 64% water, muscles and kidneys are 79%, and even the bones are watery: 31%.

At creation, all that was present was a physical sculpture. Pause and envision that! Then, God breathed out of Himself into the dormant figure His '**breath of life**'. Next, it says the figure He formed from dirt and the 'breath' He breathed *–from Himself–* into the physical clay image became something. Please observe He did **not** say the figure He formed from dirt and water became a living body; neither did He say it became a living spirit. Notice, it says, man became a living **soul**; God said the 'man' He made became a living entity. An entity is something which is self-contained and is able to function all by itself.

This makes us a **three** part being overall where **two** characteristics are expressed in **one** physical structure. "***And the very God of peace sanctify you wholly; and I pray God your whole spirit and soul and body be preserved blameless unto the coming of our Lord Jesus Christ***. I Thessalonians 5:23. According to Scripture, this parallels the **Godhead** not ~~trinity~~ which is expressed physically as Christ Jesus

The Lord. God's perfect image of Himself is Jesus in the flesh. And, He is, "***... the brightness of His glory and the express image of His person...***" Hebr. 1:3. "***For in Him dwells all the fullness of the 'Godhead' bodily.***" Colossians 2:9. The Godhead should not be viewed as; **one**- plus-**one**- plus- **one** which totals three; **1+1+1=3**. Instead, the Godhead is more accurately explained using multiples as one-times-one-times one equals "**One**"; or, **1X1X1=1**.

Our body which God made provides Him with a multifunctional vessel. It serves as both the dwelling place for the real person *–our soul–* and our eternal *–spirit–* into which He breathed life. Even in nature, we understand the reason why anyone designs a building is to accommodate someone or something of value to occupy it. When we think of a luxury hotel, library, museum, high rise building, sanctuary or bank, they are all made to fulfill specific functions. Therefore, what occupies the building or house is far more valuable and important than the structure itself.

The goal was for accommodations and storage not to be an empty or **un**occupied building. And, wherever we see intelligent **design** like a computer, car, an airplane or any beautiful construction, we subconsciously are aware there has to be a **designer**. Most of us are consciously convinced that our physical body was designed by God so that He can access the physical world. This is the reason God told us in His Word, "***For you are the temple of the living God. As God has said: I will dwell in them and walk among them. I will be their God, and they shall be My people.***" II Corinthians 6:16.

What a great privilege and distinct honor to think The Supreme Being who created the universe would choose to take up residence in humans as well? God wants to reside in a physical house simply to show us how to rule in the spiritual world as we live in the physical. Just about every successful father embraces the same outlook for their children to rule, govern and have dominion, so our Creator enjoys even greater measure of success when His offspring manages.

You see beloved, our spirit and soul are the diplomats who reside in the *–body–* house. Also, what makes a house/building valuable is its location and its content. You are located precisely where God knew you would be before the foundations of the world. And, the person who is now joined to your spirit is God's Holy Spirit to make you diverse in functionality. Great and marvelous things can take place in you for the world to see God in you and envy!

Our New Covenant says He has placed His mark of identification on each of us. "…***in whom also, having believed, you were sealed with the Holy Spirit of promise.***" Ephesians 1:13. What meticulous features and precise planning went into this detailed construction project! However, the house *–body–* can easily rule the resident if our spirit is not born a-new by the Word of God and placed back on the right track. God's Word says a change in leadership must take place so that the house –body– does not continue to exercise its dominance over its residents; our spirit and soul.

This change is also necessary in order for the body to be properly equipped to accommodate its transformed occupants. This fascinating structure *–without us doing anything–* can stop itself from bleeding if its cut, it tells you it's sick; it moves blood from its limbs to preserve the body if it gets too cold; it breathes by itself without you doing anything; it tells you it has to go to the bathroom and many other intricate functions without us having to do anything.

The Body Was Not Made to Lead Us

The apostle Paul clearly outlined to us the house should never lead us in the things of God. Instead, the body is to be subservient *–through our constant discipline–* to our mind and spirit. Furthermore, he told us how this work could be accomplished. He said, "***But I keep under my body, and bring it into subjection*** …" I Corinthians 9:27. As we know, '**I**' and '**my**' are two individual personal pronouns which denote two separate entities at work simultaneously or at the same time. To paraphrase, he was saying there is one part of me I use to exercise authority over the other part. Paul went on to explain that he could also choose where it goes, what it does and whether to engage in an activity or not. To put it another way, my transformed mind *–having now a deeper understanding of my make-up and God–* can make my body subject to the real person so God's purpose can prevail throughout my life. Today, as believers, we are aware that at times it will hurt us emotionally to deny ourselves sensual pleasures in order to carry out our Lord's will effectively. Despite how fragile we may think the house *–body–* to be, it was created by God to contain His Holy Spirit, house our spirit and to represent Him on the earth. This is a pretty awesome status which some may still take for granted.

The Bondage Associated with the Fear of Dying

The grim reality of our body is that it is constantly decaying and getting old. And, we do not know exactly how long it will live before the inevitable occurs. However, we do know, the demise of the body must occur unless there is some divine intervention by God as was evident in the case of Enoch. "***By faith Enoch was taken away so that he did not see death..***." Hebrews 11:5. Also, Elijah "…***and Elijah went up by a whirlwind into heaven***..." 2 Kings 2:11.

Within several years or decades our body will return to the ground from which it was made. This is why most people today are afraid of dying because not knowing exactly what awaits them accompanied with uncertainties will automatically result in the fear of death. In addition, the reason we fear death is because we only know life. And, very few have gone on and came back to enlighten us except Jesus. He said, ***"… I lay down my life, that I might take it again***." John 10:17.

The fear of dying is a natural human point of view. As you know, just as a pitch dark room or unfamiliar approaching loud sound can emit fear, so does the thought of the termination of physical life without assurance of what exactly is next. Moreover, if someone holds a prominent position in society, is wealthy or feels their life is very valuable, this can further contribute to the fear of dying. Very few, if any of us look forward to dying or even make provisions or plans. Approximately fifty-five 55% percent of American adults do not have a will or other estate plan in place, according to the LexisNexis site. The apostle Peter made reference to a specific reason Jesus came relevant to the bondage surrounding death. "***Inasmuch then as the***

children have partaken of flesh and blood, He Himself likewise shared in the same, that through death He might destroy him who had the power of death, that is, the devil, and release those who through fear of death were all their lifetime subject to bondage." Hebrews 2:14-15. Just as the fear of death existed and limited the potential in people's lives then, so its effect still lingers on in many lives today who are not aware of God's awesome plan. If you have never done so, we challenge you right now to hold up your hands in surrender and confess Jesus as Lord right where you are today. Let us delete the fear of death which the Word of Life refers to as bondage.

After doing so, the Scripture admonishes us to grow and increase in the knowledge of God so the fear of death does not continue to limit our God given internal gifts which we are to display to our present generation. To put it a little differently, if this state of subjection is not faced head-on, it can prevent us from ever bearing fruit designed for others to pick and enjoy. Before we acquired this knowledge of God's Word about death, most of us thought it to be the final chapter of life and the end of existence as some denominations teach.

However, as offspring we know it is simply a departure of the spirit and soul from the body to a continued state of superior existence of kings and priests unto God. "***So we are always confident, knowing that while we are at home in the body we are absent from the Lord. For we walk by faith, not by sight. We are confident, yes, well pleased rather to be absent from the body and to be present with the Lord.***" II Corinthians 5:6-8. This transition along with the increased understanding helps to bring about the assurance which will minimize and eventually eliminate the fear so commonly associated with death. Death of our body was previously thought to be a sting or something terrifying. "***O Death, where is your sting?***" 1 Corinthians 15:55.

However, to those who are in Christ, death is more of a welcomed transition as it was evident with Stephen. "***But he, being full of the Holy Spirit, gazed into heaven and saw the glory of God, and Jesus standing at the right hand of God and said, "Look! I see the heavens opened and the Son of Man standing at the right hand of God!"*** Acts 7:55-56. This transition from fear surrounding death, to the victory and enlightenment encompassing the promise of eternal life is the way death is to be viewed as children of The Most High. Only the Word of God sheds light in great detail by giving little attention to the fear of dying, as well as addressing the assurance of eternity. So while we live on earth physically, we do not have to be subjected to the fear of dying which always restricts our capabilities to carry out the great commission and works of the Lord.

"***And He said to them, "Go into all the world and preach the gospel to all creation. He who has believed and has been baptized shall be saved; but he who has disbelieved shall be condemned. These signs will accompany those who have believed: in My name they will cast out demons, they will speak with new tongues; they will pick up serpents, and if they drink any deadly poison, it will not hurt them; they will lay hands on the sick, and they will recover."***

So then, when the Lord Jesus had spoken to them, He was received up into heaven and sat down at the right hand of God. And they went out and preached everywhere, while the Lord worked with them, and confirmed the word by the signs that followed. Mark 16:15-20. By believing and acting upon His directive, we can then begin to maximize our efforts to take on challenges in the things of God, so we can wholly serve Him. "***And you shall love the LORD your God with all your heart, with all your soul, with all your mind, and with all your strength. This is the first commandment. And the second, like it, is this: 'You shall love your neighbor as yourself.' There is no other commandment greater than these***" Mark 12:30-31.

The Short Time We Have is to Be Maximized

Most of the older generation *–old-schoolers by young people's terminology–* realize life in their body is only for a few decades. This means life is very brief and valuable. Therefore, the time is not to be wasted on experimentation and fulfilling only personal desires. This is another reason God sent His Son to live on earth as our model for just thirty-three and one half (33 ½) years. It is what we choose to do with the time we have which can leave an indelible mark in the lives of others forever. God became flesh so we can observe how to live a fulfilled life. ***For in Him dwells all the fullness of the Godhead bodily***." Colossians 2:9. As you may recall, God's plan was to let people know who they are and the reason they were given life. This is so man *–the specie–* would realize their life does have a Godly purpose and should be lived righteously exhibiting a lifestyle pleasing to God. Once more, ***"Let your light so shine before men, that they may see your good works and glorify your Father in heaven."*** Mat. 5:16.

However, Jesus said, "…***The thief comes only in order to steal and kill and destroy. I came that they may have and enjoy life, and have it in abundance***." John 10:10. The primary reason for the rebirth *–covered in chapter two–* is to change man's warped conception of life to think their body only reflects needs, desires and pleasures. Jesus came to both inform and to show us how to have a better life overall here on earth in preparation for ruler-ship with Him. "***It is the Spirit who gives life; the flesh profits nothing*** …" John 6:63.

The Scripture confirms it in the book of Romans, "***so then they that are in the flesh cannot please God. But you are not in the flesh, but in the Spirit, if so be that the Spirit of God dwell in you. Now if any man have not the spirit of Christ, he is none of His***." Romans 8:8-9. A new association with the Creator and Father of our Lord Jesus Christ is transformation through His new design of rebirth.

This new union was formed to reestablish and share similar interests in meeting the needs of others. This change is designed primarily to fulfill our Godly assignment. "***The fruit of the righteous is a tree of life, and he who wins souls is wise***." Proverbs 11:30. Only when we practice a proper lifestyle of humility will we bring glory to God. "***For whoever exalts himself will be humbled, and he who humbles himself will be exalted."*** Luke 14:11.

It is evident; God is in the promotion business. Therefore, in order for this union to function effectively, a vital step of rebirth must be taken. God desires to live in our body which will bring Him glory. Again, our body becomes the only legal agency in the universe through which His authority, works and miracles will be channeled. Please note, the later in life we decide to change our direction to follow Christ, the greater the chance we will not fulfill all that He designed us to accomplish. Now we can see why it is so critical to re-commit our body today to Our Lord for His use!

The Steps in Presenting Our Bodies to The Lord

Many believers view the most critical verse in their relationship with God *–as pertaining to their body–* was recorded by the Apostle Paul in the book Romans. It reads, ***"I beseech you therefore, brethren, by the mercies of God, that you present your bodies a living sacrifice, holy, acceptable unto God, which is your reasonable service."*** Romans 12:1. These five underlined words will be our focal point for this entire chapter. Let us now delve deeply into this tremendously loaded verse. To **beseech** is to make an urgent appeal –**beg**– or request for an immediate action or deed. Do you know there are several appeals made by God to man? However, there is only one directed to our physical body.

Let's take things a step further; the word beseech literally means **to plead with a sense of urgency**. For example, in the business world we sometimes hear about a particular person, piece of equipment or upgrade which is urgently requested in order to fulfill/enhance some specific function. Urgency is always of utmost importance. This is the same immediate request God places on His offspring to present their bodies to Him. As important as it is for a business to have a special person or equipment, the Lord's plea to present our bodies to Him which far surpasses any worldly requirement. God wants to minister to the world through us, and our committed *–sanctified–* body is the only mobile vessel on the planet which He will use to accomplish His global-work.

The Presentation

As we know in Scripture, God has placed a sequence of steps for man to follow in presenting their body to Him. To **present** something means to formally introduce. Whenever we present something to anyone, it should be done with detailed consideration. Do you remember your first or most recent job interview? You prepared yourself to meet the recruiter, manager or owner. You wore your best attire to impress and to make a statement about yourself; isn't that true? And, you ladies, when you were presented with the diamond or gold engagement ring and proposed to un-expectantly, wasn't it an exciting time? Remember how you began to incorporate your left hand more in conversation and in giving directions? These memorable times are vividly remembered, frequently spoken of and are usually eternally cherished and valued.

Some people will read this book yet, will not present their body to The Lord. This is not speaking of the day when they were water baptized earlier in life or the day they confess Jesus as Lord. This is in no way intended to make you feel guilty but only to become more aware and conscious of this vital step God put in place for all His Offspring.

This commitment should also be as memorable and meaningful as other pleasant memories in your life. Guess what, if you are unsure as to when you made this required presentation, it will not hurt you to recommit your body to the Lord today. After you have done so, write the date and time in the Word of God where you will see it as a constant reminder and point of reference. Just as you keep track of anniversaries, birthdays and marriages, you are also to keep track of this defined day between you and God.

The presentation of our bodies should not be confused with the special day you confessed Jesus as Lord. "***That if you confess with your mouth the Lord Jesus and believe in your heart that God has raised Him from the dead, you will be saved. For with the heart one believes unto righteousness, and with the mouth confession is made unto salvation***." Romans 10:9-10. Once again, please refer to the diagram on page # 13 regarding your **heart**. As essential as it is to confess Jesus as Lord *–to begin the confirmation of our makeup–* it is of equal status we present our bodies to Him in order for it to function more effectively as a sanctified vessel unto Him because it is now His temple. "***Howbeit the Most High dwells not in temples made with hands***..." Acts 7:48.

The Presenting of Our Body as a Living Sacrifice

God is interested in all His children understanding His Word for the following reason. "***My people are destroyed for lack of knowledge***." Hosea 4:6. God is not in the destruction business but the re-construction field. The word '**sacrifice**' always carries the sense or outcome of a greater value. Number two; sacrifice is the giving up of something now for a more meaningful and lasting outcome later. Whenever God's children genuinely present their bodies to Him, they are offering it primarily for His service. It means, they will make a conscious effort not to yield to lust, pleasures or for our personal desires to take the lead role any longer.

As you know, we serve a holy God and He will only inhabit a living and committed entity and not reside in any other construction made by man's hand. "***However, the Most High does not dwell in temples made with hands, as the prophet says***," Acts 7:48. Therefore, we have to continue to deprive the body *–as warranted–* of worldly desires if it will re-route, obstruct or lead us once again from God into the direction of personal sinful pleasures. Hence the reason why fasting at least one day per week is so important. First, it is the healthiest thing we can do because God said we are to do it. Secondly, it provides discipline your body desperately needs.

Also, fasting helps to detoxify our body of pollutants which gives it a break from the constant processing of food. ***See Matthew 6:16-18.*** "***I fast twice in the week; I give tithes of all that I possess.***" Luke 18:12. Even today, fasting is confirmed in our medical journals as an important and healthy exercise. Beloved, our body was not equipped to process food seven days a week; it needs a day of rest. When we yield our body to temptation *–which is sin–* it will result in the breaking of fellowship and communion with the Spirit of Christ who lives in you. God does not see our body the way we do as just a physical entity, but as a living functional temple. As you know, an earthly temple is a holy place which is sanctified *–set apart–* exclusively for Godly use. Let us ask you several questions. These pertain to believers as well as non-believers.

- Would you *–being married–* have sex in the church building where believers worship on Saturday or Sunday?
- Would you paint the wall of your employer with your favorite color?
- Would you carry beer, wine or alcohol in the church or to your job and drink it?
- Would you use profanity to your parent's in their house?
- Would you deliberately lie to your wife/husband, close friend, a minister, pastor or supervisor or someone you greatly respect?
- Would you ask someone to accompany you to church to pierce a part of your anatomy?

"***Or do you not know that your body is the temple of the Holy Spirit who is in you, whom you have from God, and you are not your own? For you were bought at a price; therefore glorify God in your body and in your spirit, which are God's.***" II Corinthians 6:19-20. Beloved, if we are demonstrating maturity in our relationship with Our Father, we would <u>not</u> participate in any of the above activities. Why would some knowing better participate in things mentioned above?

The Scripture says, "***Set your affections on things above, not on things of the earth***." Colossians 3:2.

The Presenting of Our Body ***<u>Holy</u>***

"***But as He who called you is holy; you also be holy in <u>all</u> your conduct***." I Peter 1:15. And, in verse sixteen it adds, "***Be holy, for I am holy***." This is <u>not</u> just to sound spiritual, but to be intentional in our daily lifestyle. We are to conduct ourselves by exercising our Father's directives above our own. This is done by us choosing <u>not</u> to allow destructive deeds and unsafe substances to infiltrate, pierce or tattoo our body which God now calls **<u>His</u>** temple.

Again, after a firm commitment is made, the reality is, 'our' body no longer belongs to us. Therefore, we are no longer owners but occupants. God wants our body pure and committed unto Him so miracles can be funneled through it to reach others who may be in desperate need. This is why the Word of God says, "***Let not sin therefore reign in your mortal body, that ye should obey the lusts thereof. Neither yield ye your members as instruments of unrighteousness unto sin: but yield yourselves to God, as those that are alive from the dead, and your members as instruments of righteousness unto God.***" Romans 6:12-13.

God does not perform miracles, wonders and signs without belief, prayer and a willing, dedicated person(s) who choose to keep themselves properly aligned. Jesus says, "…***If anyone loves Me, he will keep My word; and My Father will love him, and We will come to him and make Our home with him***." John 14:23. God will not dwell in a vessel just to be there; something meaningful and beneficial has to emerge which will bring Him glory. In order to be effective, we are to yield the right of way to the teachings of the Holy Spirit and not just to please ourselves. "***We then that are strong ought to bear the infirmities of the weak, and not to please ourselves***." Romans 1:16

Our enemy's goal is to try to derail our trek and present easy opportunities whereby we could yield to sensual pleasures, which is guaranteed to break union with God. As a result, our pipeline can become clogged where blessings and healings do not flow through us to reach those in need. Regrettably, some believers have not grasped this truth but few have. God's ardent desire is to rescue the rest of humanity from the present state of individualism so they fuse together as one organism in Christ.

In order to be effective, we are to keep ourselves free from substances like illegal drugs, lies, gluttony, tattoos, alcohol, adultery, cigarettes, or any sexually deviation because it brings about unfamiliar spirits, darkness and deception. Remember, God refers to our body as an instrument. "***And do not present your members as instruments of unrighteousness to sin, but present yourselves to God as being alive from the dead, and your members as instruments of righteousness to God.***" Romans 6:13.

The Presenting of Our Body ***Acceptable*** *unto Him*

Most people, whether they are in business for themselves or an employee, are all familiar with this commonly used word, **acceptable**. Acceptable carries with it the intrinsic value that certain minimum standards must be met before a promotion, bonus or continued employment will be maintained. As we continue to walk in the light of God's Word, He requires growth and not dabble back into the pleasures of sin. When we confess Jesus as Lord, we become children of God. "***Behold what manner of love the Father has bestowed on us, that we should be called children of God. Therefore the world does not know us because it did not know Him***." I John 3:1.

God desires us to constantly increase in knowledge so we mirror a lifestyle well pleasing to Him. This shows evidence that He has taken up residence in us. When the apostle Paul said, … 'acceptable', it also means if our bodies are not presented to God in a joyful and pleasing way, it will not become as effective as it could be for His use. Has someone ever given you something and presented it as damaged, torn or dirty? On the other hand, when a gift was wrapped, prepared and properly presented, wasn't it highly appreciated and gladly received? And, didn't it put a smile on your face and a warm feeling in your mind?

Gifts or presents *–no matter how minute or large–* is highly appreciated because of the extent of the preparation before it was offered. Isn't it true? We are all familiar with giving or doing things and not being sincere in giving our best. And, most of us have all done many things out of obligation and guilt, but more-so out of regret and apprehension. If our disclosed motives are not acceptable by human standards, what makes us think God will accept our body for service if it is presented with hesitation or not done at all? One of the best examples of how an offering to God can make a vast difference is an account of the incident between Cain and Abel. The Scripture says, "***By faith Abel offered to God a more excellent sacrifice than Cain, through which he obtained witness that he was righteous, God testifying of his gifts …***" Hebrews 11:4.

God was appreciative at Abel's willingness to show such high regards in giving his very best. "***Abel also brought of the firstborn of his flock and of their fat. And the LORD respected Abel and his offering.***" See Genesis 4:4. Abel's gifts were of the highest quality and they were well presented to the Lord. God wants everyone to know this fact in the area of presenting our body to Him in an acceptable and respectable manner as well. The day when you decide to present your body, do it joyfully and sincerely in the name of Jesus.

Understanding What Is Our 'Reasonable Service'

In order to properly understand what 'reasonable service' is, we are to first be aware of the major occurrence which took place on our behalf two thousand years ago. The major event was God's sacrifice of His **only begotten** Son to die for us because of His great love and desire to redeem all humans to Him. "***For God so loved the world that he gave his only begotten Son, that whosoever believeth in him should not perish, but have everlasting life***." John 3:16.

As a result, He would be able to **re**-introduce His Holy Spirit to take up residence in the lives of human beings. Our Father's plan was and still is, to provide us with the opportunity to be brought back into a common union with Him. Again, God expects us to give up pleasures of life *–especially those of the body and senses–* so His ministry and works can be effectively channeled through us to reach others. There are a whole lot of people who are hurting and need answers from God. "***Be ready always to give an answer to every man that asks you a reason for the hope that is in you***..." I Peter 3:15. The Apostle Paul was directed by the Holy Spirit to mention '**reasonable service**' because it must register in our transformed minds and be clearly understood or it will seem foolish and unnecessary.

Have you ever heard this message taught about presenting your body to God? This presentation of our body requires preparation and understanding before there can be presentation and acceptance by God. Remember, this is our "**reasonable service**" and it is our standard requirement. Once our body becomes a servant, it can fully perform any reasonable service God requires.

The Transformation Process

"***Do not be <u>conformed</u> to this world but be ye <u>transformed</u> by the renewing of you mind that you may prove what is that good and acceptable and perfect will of God.***" Romans 12:2.

Those two underlined words above, <u>conformed</u> and <u>transformed</u> can be better understood if we relate conformed to a <u>chameleon</u> and transformed to a <u>caterpillar</u>. As you know a chameleon changes to adapt or blend into its surroundings. On the other hand, a caterpillar transforms itself to become more mobile and to take flight. I wonder which one the Lord desires of us to embrace. Yes, we were all like heinous caterpillars before Christ accepted us into His kingdom and presented us with this luminous opportunity to be a light unto others who are in darkness.

Being transformed means there has to be a total make-over. Some may recall a television show called '**Extreme Makeover**.' The renovations of a house or person were done by experts in various fields. After several days or weeks, there is a complete transformation and change in appearance from foundation to pinnacle and from head to toe. This is as the Scripture says, "***Therefore if any man be in Christ he is a new creation; old things are passed away behold all things are become new.***" II Corinthians 5:17. I loved seeing the response on the faces of the viewers and family members. They saw the new and improved version for the first time. We are not to play games with God by going back and forth by yielding to sin.

The Scripture asks, "***What fruit had ye then in those things whereof ye are now ashamed? for the end of those things is death.***" Romans 6:21. Sin's only objective is to try and keep us in a revolving door of pleasures so we do not move forward effectively. Some will remain stagnant with God and refuse to change.

Once an extreme makeover of a person or house is completed it is rarely repeated. After this transformation process, it becomes the recipient's responsibility to maintain what has been renewed. We are to know God's Word, fix it in our subconscious mind and choose every day <u>**not**</u> to yield to sin. This way we are able to stay in proper alignment with God to the same degree we committed to our Jobs, manager or employer.

WELCOME INTO THE FAMILY OF GOD, STEWARD OF THE MOST HIGH! ***The grace of the Lord Jesus Christ, and the love of God, and the Communion of the Holy Spirit be with you all. Amen.*** II Corinthians 13:14.

Individual Review or Class Discussion

1—When someone comes to God, one of the **first** things He requires them to do is: ______________________________

2—Did you ever present your body to The Lord? If so, when? ______________________________ If you will do so, when? ____________

____

3—According to Scripture, your body is now called: ______________________________

____

4—Please complete Romans 12:1-2 which says, " ***I beseech you therefore*** ______________________________

____

____

5—Are there any changes you will make concerning the role your body plays in God's overall plan? ______________________________

____

6—How does **creation** vastly differs from evolution? ______________________________

____

____

7—What does the acronym **DESIGN** spell-out to you?

D-
E-
S-
I-
G-
N-

____

____

Please watch this **YouTube** video by: Dr. Kent Hovind on creation series called: "**Garden of Eden**". https://youtu.be/nbqtPqnOA_c

What now; what do you do About <u>Jesus as of today</u>?

Beloved of Abba, the greatest approach we are to embrace today is to realize God's two substantive mandates. First, we are to **<u>deny</u>** ourselves. Secondly, we are to become knowledgeable on how to **<u>minister</u>** to others "***...whoever desires to come after Me, let him deny himself....'*** Mark 8:34. And, "...***he that win souls is wise***." Proverbs 11:30. Some people are very busy with their agendas mapped-out and schedules filled weeks in advance. However, we are to devote time to recognize Jesus for who He is. Enclosed is a simple but profound **ABC-Z** praise and worship we can employ daily. **Jesus**, you are:

A-lpha and Omega
B-eginning and The End
C-hrist of God
D-oor of The Kingdom
E-mmanuel God with us
F-irst and The Last
G-od in The Flesh

H-oly One of Israel
I- Am
J-esus The Christ
K-ing (King of Kings)
L-ord (Lord of Lord)
M-ighty God
N-oon day sun (Brighter than the)

O-intment poured out
P-rince of Peace, Prince of Life, Prince of The Kings of the earth
Q-ualified to be worshipped
R-edeemer of Man
S-avior of the world
T-he Bright and Morning Star
U-pholder of all things

V-ery God
W-onderful Counselor
X= North, East, West South (News) I listen to:
Y-esterday, Today and Forever
Z-eal of The Lord

The time we spend in this devotion is never wasted, it is quality time invested in worship. The word **WORSHIP** reminds us that **Jesus** is:

W-orthy
O-f
R-espect
S-pecial
H-onor &
I-ntense
P-raise

And when we praise Him, we:

P-roclaim
R-eal
A-doration
I-n
S-incere
E-xcitement

Remember, as a child, the Kings/Magi's worshipped Jesus along with providing treasures. Matthew 2:11. As you know, the people "***worshipped Him***" Mark 5:6. Jesus is "***the visible image of the invisible God***." Colossians.1:15. He is also "***the express image of The Person***" of God. Hebrews 1:3. All the "***disciples worshipped Him***!" Luke 24:52.

"***Looking for that blessed hope, and the glorious appearing of the great God and our Savior Jesus Christ***." Titus 2:13. Let's choose to stay properly aligned with God, practice an acceptable lifestyle before Him and man so He gets the **glory**. As we have mentioned several times, "***let your light so shine before men, that they may see your good works, and glorify your Father which is in Heaven***." Matthew 5:16.

Prayer for <u>Salvation</u>

Lord, in the name of Jesus I come to you believing the Good News of your provisions made just for me; You did so before the foundations of the world. You said in Your Word, if I confess and believe in your son Jesus, I will be rescued from my path of error back to a high and secure place in You. Also, You said if I come to You, You will in no way cast me out. **Thank you Lord, for receiving me as your own!**

I raise my hands and surrender myself, my lifestyle and conversations to You. I desire Your divine guidance and instruction by Your Holy Spirit from this day forward. Teach and instruct me so I can effectively follow You, in the name of Jesus. Thank you, Father!. **See 1 Thessalonians 5:18**

2nd Prayer of <u>Recommitment</u>

Abba, Father, in the name of Jesus, I come to You. You said in Your Word –my instruction manual– about life, if I confess my sin –by stating exactly what the sin is I've committed– You are faithful and just to forgive me of my sin and to cleanse me from all ***<u>un</u>****righteousness. Help me to always keep the truth in my mind because Your Word says, I should hide Your Word in my heart –subconscious mind– so I will not sin against You.* **Psalms 119:11.** Thank you Lord!

Finally, please refer to the diagram on page # 13 regarding your real ***<u>heart</u>*** *spiritually.*

3rd Prayer The __Empowerment__ of God's Holy Spirit

Abba, Father, I come to you; I thank you that when I confess Jesus as Lord, you sealed me –Ephesians 1:13– *and now I am rightly aligned with You. I ask you to fill me with your Holy Spirit right now as Jesus, the disciples and Paul were all filled with Him. I surrender myself to you; reveal to me whom I have wronged or what I must do to correct any life I've altered by my lifestyle and my words. I do not want to stunt my growth by harboring iniquity in Your temple. Thank you, Father for Your Son Jesus who is my baptizer. Matthew 3:11.*

** __New Outlook as Of Today__ **

Let us start by stating, do not become discouraged on the first day of implementation of any of the above Godly instructions. Be assured **__His Word__** is working. God wants you to be more practical in your approach by being upfront and honest in your communion with Him. He does not want you to become legalistic but be humble in dealing with others so that **He** will exalt you. Now you can begin by saying:

*Father, in the name of Jesus, help/reveal to me how to meditate and store Your Word in me. I acknowledge you in all my ways so that I remember Scripture and begin to apply Your Word during my everyday interactions. You said, the **K.E.Y** to life is __K__eep __E__ducating __Y__ourself which I ardently desire to do from this day forward and seek to better all my **__relationships__**. I know that these are the real keys to my success. Thank you Lord, in the matchless name of Jesus.*

Pursue The Reason Why You're Here

Father, in the name of Jesus, I know my life has a divine purpose because I am now identified with You. Thank you that your angels rejoiced at my spiritual rebirth. **Luke 15:10**. *Also, I realize my life is now hidden with Christ in You.* **Colossians 3:3**. *By faith I know You have revealed to me the purpose for my existence here on the earth which is to let Your light shine through me. I thank You, from this day forward I am learning more of the reason why I was given life and my purpose for this brief stay on Your earth in the name of Jesus.*

The author's personal prayer for you the reader.

I petition Abba through his Holy Spirit *–who is now joined to your spirit–* **that you discard traditions and religion so that your mind becomes like a sponge to receive the prompting of His Awesome Holy Spirit. God sent Him to seal, empower and reside within you because you are now His offspring.** Romans 8:14. **I thank you Father for Your Spirit in the reader's life in the matchless name of Jesus.**

The Holy Spirit & AfC, Dr. PDV.

Your new confession is "**But as truly as I live, all the earth shall be filled with the glory of the Lord**." Numbers 14:21. Now let us refocus and realize the diversity and attributes about **The God-Head** you represent. **Acts 17:29, Rom. 1:29 and Col. 2:9.**

Man's Three-fold Nature and Characteristics

1	**Spirit (invisible**	**Soul (mental)**	**Body (physical**
	Gen. 1:26	**I Thess. 5:23**	**Heb. 4:12**
2	Has to be…	**Must Be…**	**Becomes the …**
3	**Born again**	**Rescued/saved**	**Temple /Holy Spirit**
	John 3:3-5	**Rom. 10:9-10**	**I Cor. 6:18**
4	**Perceives**	**Discern/learns**	**Senses the physical**
	I Cor. 2:11	**Matt12:30**	**I Cor. 6:13**
5	**Candle of The Lord**	**Most valuable asset**	**House spirit & soul**
	Prov. 20:27	**Matt. 16:26**	**Gen. 1:26**
6	**Returns to God…**	**Remains with us…**	**Returns to the dirt…**
	at death of the body	**for eternity**	**at death**
	Eccl. 12:7	**Gen.1:26/ Luke 16:23**	**Eccl. 12:7**
7	**Same outline as body**	**Determines final destiny**	**Eventually resurr'ctd**
	II Cor. 12:2	**Heb. 9:27**	**Jude 1:9, Mat. 22-33**

The Full Nature and Characteristics of the God-Head

1	**God**	**Jesus Christ**	**Holy Spirit**
2	Father	Son / Jesus	Spirit
3	Creator	Creator	Architect
	Gen 1:1	Gen. 1:26	Gen. 1:2
4	Lord	Lord	Lord
5	The Almighty	God/Mighty God	God
	Gen. 17:1	Isa. 9:6 / Rev. 1:8	Acts 5:3-4
	--	--	--
6	King & Judge	(King) of kings	Governor…Ps.22:28
7	Judge	Judge Matt. 5:22	Counselor John 14:26
	In Hebrew He is:	In Greek He is:	In Latin He is:
8	Elohim./ I am	Iesosus / I Am	Paraclete / I Am
	Exodus 3:14	Mark 14:62	--
9	Ab / Abba	Everlasting Father	Everlasting Comforter
	Matt.28:19	Isaiah 9:6	John 14:26, 16:13
10	God is Spirit	Word made flesh	Present everywhere
	John 14:24	John 1:1	Romans 8:9
	--	--	--
11	Love	Grace	Communion
	II Cor. 13:14	II Cor. 13:14	II Cor. 13:14
12	Operations	Administrations	Gifts
	I Cor:12:4-6	I Cor:12:4-6	I Cor:12:4-6
13	Teacher--I Thess. 4:9	Teacher--John 8:20	Teacher--John 14:26
14	Giver—	Redeemer—	Sealer—
	John 3:16	Gal. 4:5	Eph. 1:13
15	Spirit of God	Spirit of Christ	Spirit of Truth
	John 14:24	Rom. 8:9	John 14:17
16	Provides a gift	Provides a gift	Provides a gift
	John 3:16	Acts 2:38	Acts 8:20

The Godhead in a Condensed Capsule

1st. **God** (called **Elohim** which is a plural Hebrew word) is omniscient **G.O.D** is **G**enius **o**f **D**esign. **2nd**. **GOD** defined is = **Source/Sustainer**.

3rd. **Jesus** is God's perfect revelation of Himself in the flesh. Hebr. 1:3
4th. Also, **Jesus** is the **visible** image of the **invisible** God.
Coll.1:15, He:

5th Joins----**6th**---Justifies
Every------------Every
Sinner -----------Saint
Unto-------------Unto
Salvation---------Sanctification

7th The **Holy Spirit** is the **One** and diverse person of the **Godhead**. Also, **He** is the **Power** of God, the **Spirit** of Christ and the **Revealer** of truth.

Acknowledgements

Front/back cover from Google.com

Image on page #13 drawn by: Israel Vickers

Please direct all **comments** to: TheE3internationalGroup@gmail.com
Also, e-mail us to order additional copies, conduct financial seminars, teachings and book signing at your church or organization. Please visit amazon.com/author/afcpaul to see other books.

We also have available unique bookmarks on The **Father**, **Son** and **Holy Spirit**.

I thank God for my Godly, sincere, beautiful and supportive wife, Emma Vickers throughout the entire book writing process.

Made in the USA
Columbia, SC
17 December 2022